# HAIM E. DAHAN

# TOUCHES OF GRACE

## PHILANTHROPY AND SOCIAL
## INVOLVEMENT IN ISRAEL

*In memory of my beloved mother*
**Simcha Dahan** *z"l,*
*1936-2016*


*Her heart beat pounds in my ears*
*In my heart, the sound of her footsteps*

*Avraham Chalfi*

Touches of Grace / Haim E. Dahan

Contact: asyd@netvision.net.il
ISBN 978-1979060301

# TOUCHES of GRACE

## PHILANTHROPY AND SOCIAL INVOLVEMENT IN ISRAEL

## HAIM E. DAHAN

# Contents

# PREFACE

I do not attribute much importance to myself to the point that I should share my personal story with others. Yet, due to my social involvement with educational activities over the past decades, I deeply sense that my personal story is, to a large extent, also the story of many children who live in the social and geographical periphery of Israel. Their story — my story — is about children and adolescents who are growing up in a sad and painful socio-economic reality that is obscured to many of us. A reality that hovers like a dark cloud over the future of tens of thousands of children that come from a socio-economic background similar to mine. From many years of intensive social involvement, I know that what I went through is not a thing of the past. Unfortunately, many of Israel's children are currently coping with the same dilemmas and facing similar risks as those I dealt with as a child, which condemn them to a life of poverty and deprivation.

In its sixty-nine years of existence, Israel has made amazing progress and reached many achievements in a vast variety of fields. The originality and creativity of Israelis, which is reflected in the establishment of thousands of startup companies in almost every field, have turned Israel into a source of envy for many countries in the world and earned it the nickname "Startup Nation." Yet, alongside this rapid progress and amazing development, there has been a significant regression in education and equality. Enormous social gaps have been created, which have turned Israel into one of the countries with the highest inequality levels among the Western nations. These social gaps constitute a true risk to the Zionist enterprise.

Even though the state bears the ultimate responsibility for these social gaps, the apathy and indifference that we demonstrate toward these gaps has made us all responsible for them as well. An indifferent society lacking a sense of social solidarity and mutual responsibility — a competitive and aggressive society in which each person cares only for himself and has no compassion towards the weak and the needy — is an ill society that has lost its moral existential base and whose stability is therefore at risk. On the backdrop of a country that runs away from its social obligations and neglects many parts of society to be subject to their fate, the importance of social involvement and solidarity to build a civilized, moral, ethical and just society increases. It's clear that this social involvement cannot take the place of the government, and it doesn't release the state of its ultimate obligation to care for the wellbeing of its citizens. Moreover, the impact of social involvement — at its best level — will always be significantly less in comparison to the strength and the budget of the state. It can't be a replacement for the state in closing the social gaps and providing solutions for the national problems.

However, social involvement has importance, implications and gravity that are greater than its total scope. The level of the social involvement of the citizens is first and foremost a testimony of the health, strength and lack of indifference in society. Social action brings reparation of distortions and defects and actually compliments the activities of the state. It even increases the sense of inner well-being, satisfaction and joy for anyone who is involved in it; it has the power to enrich a person's unique sense of self and provides a deeper sense of purpose. Today, there is huge social action in Israel, and it is hard to imagine the society without the great contribution of the many non-profit organizations and the action of the social entrepreneurs behind them. Well intending organizations and dutiful, caring, open-hearted people who can't remain indifferent to these social gaps work hard, away from the spotlight, in order to turn this small place we live in to a more just and righteous place. They are the human capital and the driving force behind the active civil society, and they push and advance the well-being of the weak and needy people in society. These are people who quietly give of themselves for the sake of others, with humility, perseverance and total commitment, and through their actions they realize, on a daily basis, the vision of the prophet Isaiah: "It is to share your bread with the hungry and to take the wretched poor into your home, when you see the naked, to clothe him, and not to ignore your own kin."

It's very easy to excuse ourselves from social action by claiming that it is only for those who have the means, that it is the exclusive obligation of the state, or because of a handful of corrupt acts that have given a bad reputation to the entire sector. Yet, it is important to remember: social involvement is not only for certain people, it does not come as a replacement of the state, and the absolute majority of the people who are involved with it are honest and decent people. A strong desire for Tikkun Olam (repairing the world) and a sense of moral social duty do not require capital or superhuman efforts for an idea to take shape. Tikkun Olam is not necessarily done through a revolution or through great and grandiose actions, rather through small, humble, consistent steps, for helping to repair the world of one person is the reparation of an entire world.

I have no doubt that almost each person as he is, with no relation to his personal situation, can serve, volunteer and contribute for the sake of others, and therefore strengthen the resilience of the society that we live in. It is never too early and never too late to join the circle of giving. Volunteering, helping and giving express the best in men, and serve as good means for achieving a balanced lifestyle. Involvement for the sake of others turns us into more caring citizens and connects us to the people and to the country. Those who have experienced the great pleasure, satisfaction and meaningfulness that is in social action will have a hard time understanding how it is that many others do not partake in it, and this is in a society that has endowed humanity with the values of compassion, kindness ("Chessed") and the concept of Tikkun Olam. Social action and social involvement has the power to generate positive changes and to make the place in which we live more compassionate, ethical, moral and pleasant. Even the very thought of it is inspiring.

In light of the deep rifts in Israeli society, social action — in which we work together for the sake of a common social objective, while revealing our inner human aspect, despite the differences among us — has the power to connect and allow us to get to know the other and the different as a whole, and not as a narrow label or stereotype. The social gaps can pose a unique opportunity for us to reshape the relationships among us; transforming attitudes in which the "I" sees itself at the center with everything revolving around it, into human relationships of sharing and ethical responsiveness to the "other." Observing and dealing with the needs of the other, in his daily struggles for survival, gives us a new perspective on the truly important things and brings true meaning and a sense of purpose into our lives.

There's no doubting that social polarization, lack of tolerance, weakening of morality and large social gaps constitute a true danger to the wholeness of society in Israel. The indifference and numbness in the presence of these unbelievable gaps, which have taken hold of a wide portion of society, make one feel like perhaps it is just a matter of fate and stand in stark contrast to the value of mutual responsibility that is rooted in our heritage, which is embedded in the statement that "all of Israel are responsible for one another."

The empowering experience that I had when I was young in my encounter with Prof. Sam Bergman and the enormous implications that his good deeds had for my future, placed on me a huge responsibility to "pass on" the message and to continue to strengthen the effect of this good deed. The role that Prof. Bergman played in my life was something that I wanted to fulfill in the lives of children and youth who come from a background that is similar to mine. This desire led me to my own private acts of Tikkun Olam — and in 2004, together with my friends, we established "Ofanim," a non-profit organization for the advancement of children and youth in Israel. Within this framework, I have given lectures over the recent years to many students in universities and colleges throughout Israel, specifically about Ofanim, and about social action in general. The increased interest in social action — especially among the young generation — has been encouraging and has given me hope. During the lectures, I was asked a lot about the various issues and challenges involved in setting up social initiatives. The frequent questions led me to conduct a broad examination of the existing material on non-profit organizations, social action and philanthropy in Israel. From this examination, it came up that there is a lot of information on these topics, but this information is not uniform, and is, at times, contradictory, decentralized and confused. Also, most of the existing information is theoretical, and there is very little information based on the practical experiences of the work and the challenges that are involved. These findings and the supreme importance that I see in the values of social solidarity and mutual responsibility led me to write this book. This book is not pretending to be a one-stop shop for the entire topic of social action — which is apparently an impossible task — rather it comes to point out the significant need for social action and social involvement and to comprehensively review the field of philanthropy in Israel. In addition to this, the book discusses the major challenges involved in establishing a social initiative.

The main objectives of this book are to review the state of philanthropy in Israel, to present the main challenges involved in establishing and running a social initiative, to encourage, inspire and spur more people to join the circle of giving and social action in Israel. The information and reviews are given on the background of the story that led me to social action, with examples of the main challenges faced by my friends and me while establishing our initiative. Though many of the examples are drawn from social action experience in the education field, I believe that these challenges are relevant to most of the fields of social action, whatever it may be.

The first two chapters in this book describe the empowering "key experience" that I had during my childhood, on the background of a comprehensive review of the enormous gaps in education and in the social equality in Israel, in relationship to the rest of the world. Also, these chapters discuss the reasons and main causes of the formation of these gaps, which emphasize the importance and urgency of greater social involvement in Israel. The third chapter reviews the various motives for social action and explains the importance of a strong motive for success in social action. This chapter describes, amongst other things, the motives that led some of the leading social leaders in Israel to social involvement.

The fourth chapter deals with the main aspects of building a board of directors of a non-profit organization. This chapter discusses the importance of selecting the right and appropriate people for the administration and board of directors of the non-profit organization. The fifth and sixth chapters of the book deal with the various aspects of fundraising. They present and analyze the scope of giving in Israel and the United States and also the sources and main challenges of fundraising. The seventh chapter deals with the supreme importance of the measurement and evaluation process of social action and discusses its main elements.

Beyond the research task, the main challenge in writing this book was in finding the correct balance between the vast information and describing the experiences and the examples in establishing Ofanim. I hope that I have succeeded, even if just a little bit, in this effort. If this book should cause even a small handful of good people to join the circle of social action in Israel — that will be an ample return for my humble work.

# CHAPTER ONE:

# THE BEGINNING
# OF THE JOURNEY

*Give me a fulcrum, and I shall move the world.*

- Archimedes

# 1.

## A VISIT TO THE UNIVERSITY

On one hot and humid day in July, during the summer vacation of 1974 when I was 14 years old, I had a random encounter that would completely change the course of my life. After aimlessly wandering around Be'er Sheva on an old and rusty bicycle, I returned home, thirsty and drenched in sweat, to escape the oppressive desert heat and to quench my thirst. When I got home, I was surprised to find in my house that the table was set with my mother's most delicious delicacies spread out on it and a pair of unfamiliar guests sitting and eating to their heart's content. The surprising silence in the house was in stark contrast to the typical noise and commotion of a house that bustled with the life of a family of ten children.

It seemed that the absence of my nine brothers and sisters is what motivated my mother to invite me to join our guests at the tempting table, as due to our meager resources it was typical in our house that only the adults would dine with guests. I really enjoyed that tasty meal that I just happened upon and the full attention that I received from everyone there. From the simple conversation that we had, I understood that the woman and my mother had met in the community center where they both worked — the guest as a ballet teacher and my mother as a cook. The woman explained that she was already familiar with my mother's delicious cooking and that she loved it so much that she had to bring her husband Sam to taste it so that he could understand what she was talking about. Sam Bergman was apparently a well-known professor of computer sciences in the United States. As he was a passionate Zionist, he decided to immigrate to Israel with his family in order to strengthen and contribute to the young and developing country. Sam was one of the founders of the computer sciences department at the young Ben-Gurion University, where he served as a professor.

Sam had a fatherly look, and his appearance reminded me of the famous scientist, Albert Einstein. His forehead was high and furrowed, his graying hair was long and pulled back and his wise blue eyes squinted in their sockets. While he enjoyed the steaming hot dishes, he asked me about what I was doing with myself. Amongst other things, he asked me if I knew what computers were. Since I answered no, he then asked me if I would be interested in learning about them and proposed that I visit the university, where he would give me a personal introduction to computers. The offer fascinated me, and we set it up to meet the next day at the computer lab of the university.

As soon as Sam and his wife left, I began to yearn for the visit. I knew the university buildings only from a distance, through the school bus windows during my many rides to school. The university always looked to me like a picture from another planet. In my mind's eye, I saw it as a distant and special place, reserved for people of a different kind, a sort of Olympus where the gods dwell. Therefore, at the time, I couldn't stop imagining what it would look like on the inside, and the thought that I would pass through its gates really excited me and made me full of pride. As far as I knew, none of my siblings or friends in the neighborhood had ever visited there, and I was filled with a sense of self-importance over the privilege to be a pioneer.

The next day, I got up early, put on my best clothes and at the determined time, I arrived at the gates of the university. I presented myself at the main gate and asked the guard where the computer lab was located. To this day, I still remember the great excitement that gripped me while I was walking there for the first time. It seemed like the passage through the gates of the university was like a passage between two worlds: from the world of my neighborhood that was small, crowded, familiar, lacking in order and discipline, a world that was sometimes tempting and dangerous — to the big wide world that was somewhat alienated, yet orderly, clean and secure. I was amazed by the enormous open courtyards, the green lawns, the large buildings and the many students who were spread out in groups all over the campus. The atmosphere was magical, and a sense of mystery surrounded what was happening in the classrooms and laboratories.

I floated like I was in a dream toward the computer lab, where I found Sam. He was sitting in front of a large, square computer screen with a bulky keyboard in front of him, waiting for me. Barefoot and with a big smile, he pulled another chair over and invited me to sit. I was thrilled to be in a room that was lined with rows of computers, and also by the unique and magical atmosphere that hovered there. In his thick American accent, with a tender, warm smile and endless patience that I had never encountered before then, he explained basic computer concepts to me: processors, monitors, keyboards, CPU, operating systems, programming language and other concepts that sounded in my ears like magic words. Every so often, students would come to Sam with questions, and he gently and thoroughly answered them, happily and politely. I was surprised by the friendly relationship between him and the students and from his unmediated accessibility. There was something in this nice man that captured the heart of anyone who encountered him. The great and true love that Sam had for people emanated from him, and it was easy to see the respect and admiration that the students had for him, a respect and admiration that I also feel to this day for this special man.

After two hours that flew by, my introductory lesson to the world of computers came to an end, and Sam and I set it up to meet in the same place, at the same time the next week. I walked slowly on my way out of the university with a rare sense of exaltation, taking in the sights and atmosphere of the campus. To my joy, my fate had taken a turn for the better and I merited to five more weekly meetings with Sam, which were each two hours long. I don't remember what exactly I learned during those wonderful meetings, and it seems that the details themselves are not important. The important thing is the huge influence that these meetings had on the direction my life would take. During that time, I even understood that the passage through the gates of the university was not just a physical passage, but also a passage of my consciousness that shattered artificial barriers and limitations that I had unconsciously imposed on myself.

The many reinforcements that I received from Sam, along with the recognition that the students that I had encountered during my six visits at the university were ordinary people just like me, instilled in me the courage to formulate the idea that if I really wanted to, perhaps I could also study in the university one day. This thought had been a totally foreign concept to me prior to my meetings with Sam, and it gradually started to take root in me. Over time, it turned into a goal, and I was determined to prove to myself and to the world that I was indeed capable of being a full-fledged university student. The great importance I had associated with the meetings with Sam and the tremendous change they initiated in me also occupied me for many years afterward. I really wanted to understand what it was about those meetings that so greatly influenced me. What was the secret of their charm and power?

A few years ago, I came across the book by Prof. Gad Yair, On the Power of Education: From Key Experiences to Turning Points.[1] For me, this book brought to light the meaning of that experience that I had during my childhood, and in a certain way, it gave me part of the answer to the riddle. Apparently, the meeting with Prof. Sam Bergman and also the passage through the gates of the university, had created for me what Prof. Yair terms as a positive "key experience." Yair claims in his book that many people have intense and unusual experiences like these.

He writes, "In many cases a short, single educational activity is enough to create a very meaningful key experience in the biography of those who participate in it." From a study of over 3,000 key experiences in more than 1,000 Israeli adults, it became clear to the team of researchers lead by Prof. Yair that such key experiences impact the lives of people in many areas of their life, not just in academic achievements. The key experiences influence the participants' personalities, values, choice of profession and field of study and also the way they think and their worldview. "Many of these experiences happened all at once, in a one-time activity in which the level of psychological arousal reached an unprecedented peak. There was great excitement, enthusiasm, ecstasy, love, a sense of enlightenment and revelation," he writes.

Prof. Yair goes on to explain that many of the key experiences happen during the routine course of life, without prior planning of the activity and its impact. It is difficult or even impossible to plan a key experience: each individual from the groups of people, according to his identity and his needs, may grasp the same experience differently. The experience could be powerful and positive for one person, while for others it could have no impact at all. In this aspect, I felt that I was lucky that my meetings with Prof. Bergman, in the timing and the circumstances in which they occurred, turned into a positive and empowering key experience for me. The impression that the positive key experience of my childhood had left in me resonated and significantly impacted me in almost every aspect of my life. One of the thoughts that preoccupied me for a long time was regarding the chance of the encounter. Was the change in my life random? Was it pure "luck"? What would have happened had I not met Prof. Bergman?

The British film Sliding Doors, directed by Peter Howitt, demonstrates how a small deviation, seemingly coincidental, in the course of one's life can create an extreme and substantial change in the lives and identities of those who participate in the event.

Was my encounter with Prof. Bergman just a sliding door among the variety of possible courses of my life? I've pondered this again and again. There is a variety of possible answers to this philosophical question. Our holy sages claim that, "Everything is foreseen, and free will is given, and with goodness the world is judged, and all is in accordance to the majority of the deed."[2] Max Born, winner of the Nobel Prize in Physics, nevertheless claimed that "there are only two possibilities: that we believe in absolute determinism and relate to free will as a subjective illusion, or that we take the mystical approach and treat the laws of science as a meaningless illusion."[3] Prof. Gad Yair and his team of researchers say that in regards to the key experience — it seems coincidental only at first glance, but through a precise scientific analysis of these experiences, "there is a repeating consistency in them." In his opinion, there are common circumstances in these experiences, and they indicate "the conditions that enable the establishment of a turning point in the biography of those who participate in them and the psychological mechanisms that are activated in the key experiences, especially the process of self-discovery in whoever experiences them."

It's difficult to properly appreciate the huge potential of the impact that a key experience can have on a child or an adolescent without acknowledging the environment that he is growing up in. Many of the children and adolescents in the disadvantaged neighborhoods and the geographical and social periphery in Israel grow up in an environment in which their parents are new immigrants struggling to acclimate to the new country, with its different culture and foreign language. These parents sometimes "get lost" and along the way also lose their status, and the clear familial hierarchy, which they had been accustomed to for generations in their original country, is undermined. Parents who have different cultures and languages, who are invested in daily survival, sometimes become irrelevant in the eyes of their children. In many cases, the irrelevance of the parents creates a backward and unnatural dependency of the parents on their children, and their parental authority completely dissipates. Children who grow up in an environment like this are forced to mature overnight and make fateful decisions about their futures, without any of the direction or experience that is gathered in a normal process of maturity. These children have no past to lean on and no future to dream about. They are dependent on the here and now like an acrobat walking a tightrope, and any light breeze can determine their fate for better or for worse. When there is no positive role model or responsible adult at home, the child is completely exposed to the influence of his environment.

So, it's no wonder that many of my childhood friends

— smart and clever children who are full of potential — were exposed to negative influences that destroyed their futures and condemned them and their children to a life of ignorance, poverty and deprivation. In the environment that I grew up in, negative key experiences have the power to pull a child or adolescent into difficult situations whose endings are unknown, while positive key experiences could serve as an Archimedean point, which with the slightest push can trigger the process that will unleash the power that is inherent in the child and will ultimately create a great positive change in his future. These children who come from a background of deprivation have a tremendous hunger for success. This hunger, which cannot be satiated, can serve as an additional driving force and gives them a huge advantage in coping with what the future has in store for them. The idea that a short, even one-time event has the potential to generate such a vast change in someone's life is an idea that is encouraging, hopeful and inspiring.

There is no doubt that what helped us — my siblings and me — not to stray from the right path was my mother's great concern for us and her watchful eye that looked out for us at all times. Though she was unable to study during her childhood, she passed her curiosity on to us and instilled in us the understanding that academic studies are the key to a better future. "Had I been able to, I would have sold my own two eyes so that you could be able to study," she would say to us, but her need to take care of ten children left her with no choice. Also, her lack of orientation in Israeli culture and in the vital requirements of higher learning, and her inability to help us advance in academics — turned the possibility of academic studies for us into a distant and unachievable dream. On this backdrop, it is possible to understand the powerful impact that my positive key experience had on my life, and indirectly on the life of my younger siblings. This experience bridged the enormous gaps in my consciousness and made the possibility of higher learning something that could be fulfilled.

# 2.

## FOLLOWING THE KEY EXPERIENCE

In order to achieve the goal that I set for myself — to study in the university — I had to jump a few hurdles. The first — a necessary condition, though not enough to get accepted into university — was to graduate high school with a full matriculation certificate. This was not at all simple; after one year of learning in a high school in Be'er Sheva, I happened to transfer in 10th grade to a Bnei Akiva Yeshiva boarding school. The education I received at the high school in Be'er Sheva was at a lower level than the level of education in the yeshiva, and so the huge gap between me and the other students in the boarding school caused the mathematics teacher to basically give up on me. One day he simply said to me, "It seems to me that you won't be able to take the final mathematics matriculation exam, so there's no point in you even coming to classes." Following my encounter with Prof. Bergman, I understood that I must study mathematics and get a good score on the final exam in order to get accepted to university. Therefore, when I returned to the boarding school after the summer vacation, I approached the mathematics teacher and explained to him that I was insisting on coming to class and that I promised to work hard in order to catch up. I could see his lack of faith in his face, but fortunately, he did not object.

Thus, I began to study on my own during the evenings in order to narrow the enormous gap. I wanted to do the same for my level of English, so I approached the English teacher and asked what I needed to do to get accepted into the top English group and take the English matriculation exam. He recommended that I read short English booklets. So, I started to invest most of my free time in catching up in mathematics and English, which, at first, had seemed to me like an impossible task. Yet, through hard work, perseverance and determination, I started to catch up. Approximately six months later, I began to see the fruit of my labor. The significant improvement in the scores on my tests and exams encouraged me to continue to work hard and improved my sense of being able to do it. I felt like my academic success was primarily dependent on me and my willingness and ability to work hard. The academic success even improved my social status at the boarding school.

In retrospect, the easiest and most simple thing to do would have been to simply give up on the mathematics and English matriculation and "gain" a few more free hours, which I surely would have used to play soccer or basketball, or to just do nothing. Yet, the huge curiosity that my mother had instilled in me, and the strong faith that Prof. Bergman had in me, made me insist on studying these subjects and stick to it. In a certain sense, my insistence was fundamental and decisive for my future. Meaning, during that period I lived in a boarding school away from home. My parents and my older siblings were not involved in my studies at all. As opposed to me, my older siblings had to drop out of school at a young age to help provide for the family.

My parents' lack of interest did not come from their lack of caring, rather from a lack of awareness that mostly stemmed from their lack of higher education. Lack of parental awareness in regards to the importance of academics and their inability to direct, assist and advance their children — are among the main obstacles in narrowing the gaps in education. Without this parental awareness, the gaps between the children of parents who are uneducated (or have a low-level of education) and the children of parents with a higher education — only continue to widen. Educated parents have awareness. They urge, push and instill in their children the understanding of the importance of an education for success in life. On the other hand, the children of uneducated parents, who receive from them very limited support, advice and assistance, are dependent mainly on themselves.

Also, educated parents generally have more prestigious professions than the parents that have no or little education. So, it's no wonder that there is a clear correlation between the prestige of the father's job and the likeliness of earning a matriculation certificate. Findings show that between 1995 and 2008 the chances of high school students receiving a matriculation certificate greatly increased, however, this is especially seen primarily among the students whose parents have occupations that are considered to be prestigious and have a higher education. This means that the growth in the rates of earning matriculation certificates are accompanied by the considerable growth of inequality between the various classes of society.[4]

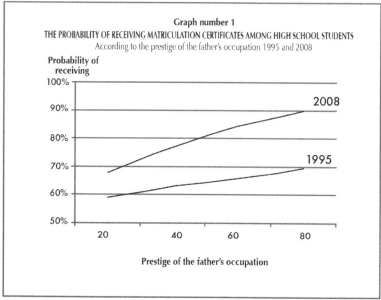

**Graph number 1**
THE PROBABILITY OF RECEIVING MATRICULATION CERTIFICATES AMONG HIGH SCHOOL STUDENTS
According to the prestige of the father's occupation 1995 and 2008

Probability of receiving

2008

1995

Prestige of the father's occupation

Source: Bar Haim, Blank and Shavit, Taub Center
According to the ISEI index (1=low, 100=high)

My parents were simple, innocent, honest, God-fearing people, and in their own humble way, they provided for me and my siblings a childhood that was spiritually rich and poor in material. They were occupied with the hardships of making a living, and they had no references and no ability to take an interest in my studies. My father worked very hard his entire life as a simple construction worker. In order to help support her family, my mother also went out to work once her young children got older. She was a cook in the neighborhood community center, where, as I mentioned, she met Prof. Bergman's wife. The positive key experience that I had during my childhood compensated in a certain way for my parents' lack of awareness, and it pushed me and helped me focus on one goal: to reach the university. And indeed, through hard work and determination, I succeeded in completing my high school studies and received a complete matriculation certificate.

A few months prior to the completion of my military service, without any preparation, I took the university acceptance exams. I simply took a special one-day vacation from the combat unit that I was serving in, took the exams and immediately returned. In retrospect, it seems like there is great naivety and even ignorance in a move like that, a move that stems from a lack of awareness and a lack of guidance and advice. But in those days, preparatory courses for university acceptance exams were not so common. And even if they were, it's very likely that I wouldn't have been able to pay for them with my meager resources. Today there are a few private schools that prepare students for university acceptance exams, but these preparatory courses are especially expensive, and this constitutes an additional barrier for young people from a low socio-economic background.

Along with taking the acceptance exams, I submitted registration forms to Ben Gurion University. In the section where I had to fill in the three fields of study that I was interested in, by order of preference, I wrote only "computer science." I simply didn't know about anything else. What I really wanted was to be a full-fledged student in the department of mathematics and computer sciences where

Prof. Bergman was teaching. The truth is that I was very worried that my academic adventure would end with that registration. Each day following my registration, I would go with great apprehension to the mailbox to check whether I had received an answer from the university. I was convinced that the answer would be negative. In the end, when the long-awaited letter finally arrived, I was scared to open it. When I did open it, to my joy and surprise, I saw that I had been accepted to study in the mathematics and computer sciences department of Ben Gurion University, just as I had hoped, wanted and dreamed of. I was gripped by immeasurable excitement and pride.

An invitation was attached to the university letter of acceptance to come, along with all of the other new students, to a day for counseling and to build the class schedule a few weeks before the start of the academic year. I was yearning for the day to come that I would meet Prof. Bergman again, who was noted in the letter as one of the academic advisors. Since we hadn't seen each other since our initial meetings in the computer lab, I was really excited to tell him that I had gotten accepted into the department of the university where he was teaching. It seemed like Sam was even more excited than I was, and he invited me out to lunch that same day. We sat together for a few hours and I was full of great excitement and a tremendous sense of satisfaction. In his sensitive and modest way, he helped me understand that I was not alone, that he would always be there for me should I need any guidance, support or assistance. Just that idea alone made me feel calm and secure.

After getting accepted into the university, I was discharged two weeks early from the mandatory three-year minimum required army service so that I could immediately begin my studies. The transition from the army to studying was very sudden: I returned my army equipment to the base on Thursday, and on the following Sunday I was already standing proudly in my first day at the university campus. At the start of the academic year, I strolled between the classrooms and auditoriums with a sense of elation, yet after only a few days, it hit me that in order to complete my degree I would have to study and work really hard. I also needed to think about where I would find the money to cover the high tuition. To do that, along with a packed schedule of classes, I had to take side jobs in landscaping, painting and substitute teaching in various high schools throughout Be'er Sheva.

The financial, cultural and cognitive gaps that exist between the strong and the weak classes of society are also among the causes of the gaps in utilizing educational opportunities. As we saw, it's no secret that there is a tight connection between the parents' socio-economic status and the academic level of the children. Yet, this connection has absolutely nothing to do with ability and potential, which exist equally in every group of people.

The current situation is mostly due to a lack of finances, guidance, parental awareness and expectations that the child will progress academically. The children of uneducated parents who have achieved their bachelor's degree typically feel that, in relationship to their parents, they have achieved "enough." On the other hand, the children of parents with an academic education will most likely follow in their parents' footsteps and even go further than that. My academic studies were an act of pioneering and were a deviation compared to my family and my environment. Yet, for my children, academic studies are already a natural direction to go in. Studies show that the reform of the matriculation exams and higher education in the 1990's and 2000's contributed to a significant increase in education rates, yet it also contributed to a significant increase in educational inequality between the classes of society.[5]

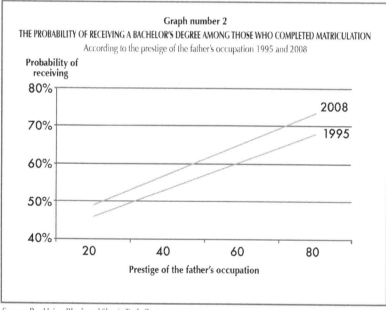

**Graph number 2**
THE PROBABILITY OF RECEIVING A BACHELOR'S DEGREE AMONG THOSE WHO COMPLETED MATRICULATION
According to the prestige of the father's occupation 1995 and 2008

Source: Bar Haim, Blank and Shavit, Taub Center
According to the ISEI index (1=low, 100=high)

In 1984, after I successfully completed my bachelor's degree in mathematics and computer sciences, I was interested in working in the field of computers, and I sent my resume to a few companies. In the interview at the Be'er Sheva office of the Dead Sea Works company — where I got my first job with a bachelor's degree in computers, as a programmer — they explained to me the duties of the position and the terms that accompanied it. The base salary that they offered me was 1,600 shekels per month. It was a reasonable starting salary, but not particularly high for the field of programming. After I finished the interview, I went to visit my father at the construction site where he was working, which was not far from where the interview had taken place. It was early in the afternoon, and my father and his coworkers had just sat down for lunch on the construction site. My father was extremely happy to see me, and in his modest way, he immediately offered me his lunch. I told him that I wasn't hungry, and I even lied to him, telling him that I had just eaten since I knew that it was the only way to prevent him from insisting. In the end, he let it go but still insisted on making me a cup of tea.

He handed me his pay stub and asked me to read it. When I opened the pay stub, I was amazed to see his monthly salary — including overtime — a total of 360 shekels. This was my father's salary as a construction worker with 33 years of seniority in the construction company that he worked for. I felt a harsh burn in the presence of the enormous gaps. I, who just got accepted to my job, would be making four and a half times more than my father is making after 33 years of harsh and difficult work. Still, despite his low salary, my father never complained about his work and he always defended the company that employed him with great fervor. He felt like it was a great privilege that he was able to provide a livelihood for his family with dignity. "May God bless them, it is in their merit we have food on the table," he would typically say about the company that employed him. I never understood where my father drew his enormous innocence and his strong and pure faith from. In many ways, my father was the richest man that I've ever met in my life — the person who was truly and genuinely happy with his portion.

After I finished studying for my bachelor's degree, I felt like I must personally thank Prof. Bergman for his decisive contribution to this achievement of mine. We sat together on the balcony of his house, looking out at the view of the Negev Desert, enjoying a cold beer. During the conversation, he asked me, "So, what are you going to do now?" I answered that I intended to gain a little experience in my new temporary job, and after that, I'd try to find a permanent job in the field. He asked, "Why not continue studying?" I answered that I see my bachelor's degree as a great and satisfying achievement, "especially in light of the fact that my father never studied and in light of the fact that my older brothers didn't even finish high school." Sam was very surprised by my answer. After a few moments of silence, he asked, "What does the level of your father's and brothers' education have to do with you? Why are you binding yourself with artificial chains?" I again felt the lack of authority and parental guidance that I thought I had reconciled with in the first years of my university studies. This sentence also echoed through my head for a few days after that.

The perspective that Sam had presented stunned me

and wouldn't let go of me: most of the restrictions that we have are artificial. A lot depends on us and only on us, and if we believe in ourselves, and if we take responsibility for our future, we can go far.

Our origin and our starting point do not need to be chains or constraints on our dreams and our fantasies. A few weeks later, I registered to study for a master's degree, which I successfully completed in 1987. Prof. Bergman's guidance had compensated for my previous lack of awareness, strengthened my self-confidence, and increased my odds against the sheer statistic — that left me with slightly more than a ten percent chance of achieving a master's degree.

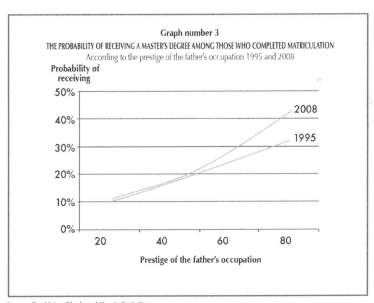

**Graph number 3**
THE PROBABILITY OF RECEIVING A MASTER'S DEGREE AMONG THOSE WHO COMPLETED MATRICULATION
According to the prestige of the father's occupation 1995 and 2008

Source: Bar Haim, Blank and Shavit, Taub Center
According to the ISEI index (1=low, 100=high)

The sheer statistic that is shown in the graphs above embodies a painful and sad reality, which many of us are not aware of. This reality hovers like a black cloud over the future of tens of thousands of children who come from a socio-economic background similar to that in which I grew up. Following the many years of my intensive social involvement in the social and geographical periphery in Israel, I know that what I personally went through is not a thing of the past. Also today, many of Israel's children are currently coping with the same dilemmas and are facing the same risks that I dealt with as a child. To a large extent, the gaps in education between the lower and upper classes of society have become even wider and deeper today, and the chance that these children will escape the statistic that condemns them to a life of poverty and deprivation is very slight. This is a situation that I am not sure that the State of Israel can withstand for very long.

# CHAPTER TWO:

# THE SOCIETY IN ISRAEL, A LOOK FROM INSIDE

*You and I, we'll try from the beginning*
*it will be tough for us, no matter, it's not so bad.*
*Others have said it before me but it*
*doesn't matter - you and I we'll change the world.*

- Arik Einstein

# 1.

## THE GAPS IN EDUCATION AND SOCIAL EQUALITY

The state's economy has experienced much turbulence since its establishment; among them have been hyper-inflation, the bank stock crisis, the Arab boycott and many wars. Despite these difficulties, the financial reforms that were instituted by the Israeli governments in the last few decades, the tremendous technological developments and the development of the high-tech market have all led to a high level of advancements and economic growth that is beyond impressive. During recent years, the economic growth is reflected in the State of Israel's surplus in the current account on the balance of payments, a significant drop in debt-to-Gross Domestic Product (GDP) ratio, low budget deficits and a consistent increase in labor market participation.

The GDP in Israel grew from 963,680,000,000 shekels (approx. 440 billion USD) in 2006 to 1,486,213,000,000 shekels (approx. 580 billion USD) in 2015.[1] As a result, foreign investors, world banks and world credit rating agencies express great confidence in the strength of the Israeli economy. Along with Israeli entrepreneurship, fearlessness, imagination, innovation and chutzpah, the strength of the economy has led to an endless stream of companies from around the world knocking on Israel's doors asking them to set up development centers and to buy or invest in Israeli start-up companies and cutting-edge technologies.

In the 69 years of the existence of the state, Israel has made remarkable achievements in a vast variety of fields: agriculture, manufacturing, technology, medicine, research, security, etc. Creativity and originality have turned Israel into a source of envy for many people in countries all over the world, and even earned it the nickname "The Startup Nation." These achievements especially stand out on the backdrop of the unique challenges that Israeli society has faced: the absorption of enormous waves of immigration (more than 37% of the population are immigrants) and the economic implications of the ongoing Arab-Israeli conflict, which is reflected in high security expense. Yet, along with the huge economic progress and development, there are two essential areas in which there has been total failure: education and social equality.

Education is the cornerstone of building a society, and one of the most effective tools for closing social gaps and striving for equality. Education plays an important role in determining the individual's level of income and quality of life, and in determining the level of the socio-economic development of the country as a whole. The saying "Education is power" is really reflected in reality; a high level of education strengthens self-confidence and financial security. There is a close connection between the level of education and the rate of employment and income level. These gaps are especially evident during financial crises. The impact of the level of education on the prospect of employment increased following the world economic crisis that started in 2008.

A survey by the Organization for Economic Co-operation and Development (OECD) from 2013 shows that from 2008 to 2011 the unemployment gap between those with low education levels and those with high education levels widened in all of the organization's member countries. In all of the age groups, the rate of unemployment among those with a low education rose by almost 3.8 percent, compared to a rise of 1.5 percent among those with high education levels.[2] In Israel as well, the large gaps in the unemployment rate and income distribution are related to the lack of suitable skills for the labor market and especially to the lack of higher education.[3]

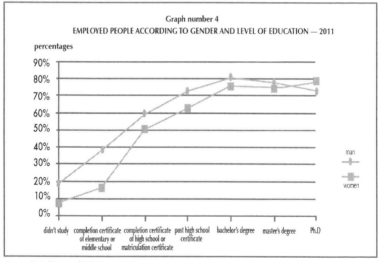

Source: Central Bureau of Statistics

The quality of education is especially important for the State of Israel, as human capital is its main resource. The importance of education is well reflected in the OECD data, which shows that the return on education in the Israeli labor market is higher than the average in developing countries.[4] During the last few decades, there has been a consistent and concerning drop in the results of the educational system in Israel, in spite of the increase in the country's education expenditures, and the new education reforms in the education system in Israel.[5] Results of the PISA (Program for International Student Assessment) from 2015 show that the achievements of ninth and tenth-grade students in Israel in the areas of science, literacy and mathematics were significantly lower than their counterparts in most of the OECD countries. These examinations also showed that the gaps in achievements between the rich and the poor and Jews and Arabs are expanding and are disturbing. Since 1999, the achievements of socio-economically weak Israeli children are significantly lower than the achievements of the weak students in the OECD countries.[6,7]

Also, in the Trends in International Mathematics and Science Study (TIMSS) comparative international research of 2015 — which examines the level of knowledge in content and cognitive skills of eighth graders from 39 countries around the world — there is significant regression of Israeli students' achievements in mathematics and science as compared to 2011. This research showed that there are large gaps in these two areas of knowledge between the different sectors as well as between students with a strong financial background and students with a weak financial background.[8] You can see that in Israel itself, the gaps between the achievements of students from cities in the high socio-economic strata and the achievements of students from cities in the low socio-economic strata are only widening.[9]

In most established cities, along with the public education system, a private education system has developed in which parents pay for private tutoring for their children. In a short, non-scientific survey that I conducted in a high school in an established city in the Sharon region, it turns out that 90 percent of the students were partaking in private tutoring lessons that their parents were paying for. This is in addition to an abundance of extra-curricular activities and enrichment classes that the established local municipalities offer, in comparison to the meager supply offered by the socio-economically weak municipalities. The development of a private education system in well-established cities draws good teachers to those cities from all over Israel who work as teachers in the public schools, while some of them give private lessons after school hours. This phenomenon creates a situation where the quality of the teachers in the weak social and geographical periphery continues to decrease.

The phenomenon of private tutoring even leads to enormous gaps between the center of the country and the periphery in the number of twelfth-grade students who take the matriculation exams at a 5-unit level (the highest level), something that is an advantage for getting accepted to study engineering and sciences. For example, in 2014, 201 students from well-established Ramat Hasharon (with 44,000 residents) took the mathematics matriculation exams at a 5-unit level — as compared to only two (2) students from the southern peripheral city of Kiryat Malakhi (with 24,000 residents). In order to succeed in the matriculation exam, students must invest a very great deal of effort, and a private tutor significantly helps.[10] But private lessons cost money, which is something that few people in the social and geographical periphery can afford.

### TABLE 1

## The amount of examinees in mathematics at a level of 5 study units
*center vs. periphery (2014)*

The top ten cities

| | |
|---|---|
| Ramat Hasharon | 25.00% |
| Herzliya | 24.18% |
| Ra'anana | 19.27% |
| Ramat Gan | 18.92% |
| Kiryat Ono | 18.72% |
| Givatayim | 17.86% |
| Haifa | 17.61% |
| Kfar Saba | 15.75% |
| Kiryat Tivon | 15.67% |
| Modiin — Macabim Reut | 15.51% |

## The lowest ten cities

| | |
|---|---|
| Tiberius | 5.30% |
| Beit Shemesh | 5.00% |
| Akko | 4.80% |
| Tayibe | 4.38% |
| Shfaram | 4.08% |
| Netivot | 3.81% |
| Ramle | 2.91% |
| Tzfat | 2.73% |
| Rahat | 1.54% |
| Kiryat Malakhi | 0.82% |

*Source: Ynet website, May 2016*

The small number of students that take matriculation exams at the 5-unit level and the negative implications of that for the economy led the Ministry of Education to embark on an aggressive journey in 2016 to increase the number of students who take this matriculation exam. This journey brought an impressive rise in the number of twelfth-grade students who took the 5-unit matriculation exam: from 10,804 in 2015 to 12,800 in 2016.[11] However, most of the additional 5-unit graduates came from schools in well-established cities. The enormous gaps in education between the low and high social classes also led to supplementing budgets and placing an emphasis on the studies of mathematics, English and the sciences in the periphery in 2016. The results of Meitzav exams (measuring school effectiveness and growth) for the 2015-2016 academic year indicated an improvement in relationship to the 2014-2015 academic year between children from a low socio-economic background and children from a high socio-economic background, in everything related to science and technology, Hebrew and mathematics.[12] Narrowing the enormous gaps — gaps that stem from years of extensive negligence — is a long and slow process that requires additional budgets, persistence and perseverance. The slight improvement between 2014-2015 and 2015-2016 is a small step in the right direction, but there is still a long road ahead to closing the gaps to reasonable and acceptable levels.

Regarding the Arab sector, the gaps are even larger, and you can easily see the discrimination and the ongoing negligence by the state in development budgets, education budgets, etc. These gaps make their mark on the achievements of students in this sector as compared to their counterparts in the Jewish sector. These gaps are increasing to shameful levels in the Bedouin sector, where the neglect and poor conditions are a badge of poverty for the State of Israel: the amount of students who took the five-unit exam in mathematics in the Bedouin sector is especially low and swayed between 2.0 percent in 2010 and 3.3 percent in 2014. More than 50 percent of the Arab examinees and all of the Bedouin examinees learn in schools that are defined as having a high educational deficit (a weaker population). In 2014, only two percent of the examinees in the Arab sector studied in schools that are defined as having a low educational deficit (i.e., a strong population). On the other hand, more than half of the examinees in the Jewish sector learn in schools that are defined as having a low educational deficit.[13]

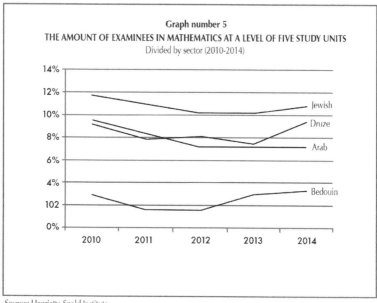

**Graph number 5**
THE AMOUNT OF EXAMINEES IN MATHEMATICS AT A LEVEL OF FIVE STUDY UNITS
Divided by sector (2010-2014)

Source: Henrietta Szold Institute

From a close examination of the successful education systems in OECD member states, which was performed by McKinsey et al., it came up that one of the main parameters for success in education is the quality of the teachers in the classrooms.[14] The low status and salary of teachers in Israel is an indication of a lack of appreciation and lack of internalization of the importance of the profession, and therefore makes it more difficult to recruit quality labor to the system. Students from well-established families who live in strong municipalities enjoy high-quality teachers, private tutors, an abundance of extra-curricular activities and enrichment lessons that are offered by the local municipality, hence causing the gaps in educational achievements between them and the students in the geographical and social periphery to continue to widen.

Another trait that is also important to the gap in education between the students of the different socio-economic cross-sections is the lack of parental awareness. Educated parents read about, are interested in and are aware of the different possibilities for enriching their children and helping them advance. While many of the uneducated parents are mostly occupied with the day-to-day financial struggle and don't have the time and space to think about additional ways of pushing their children to advance towards better achievements.

The gaps in education directly affect the gaps in society and deepen the inequality in Israeli society in a significant and dangerous way. On this backdrop, it is important to remember that during the first decades of the establishment of the state, Israel proudly and gloriously led the list of socially egalitarian countries. Paul Anthony Samuelson, the Nobel prize-winning Jewish American macro-economist, wrote in his canonical book, Economics: An Introductory Analysis: "Which country is the most egalitarian today?... if we limit ourselves to the Western world, the possibility has been raised that the new country, Israel, perhaps stands at the top of the list."[15]

Those were the days of innocence for this young and developing country. From the middle of the 1980's, the Israeli economy went through a transformation, from a centralized socialist economy with a broad public sector and a large tax burden, towards a more competitive market economy. Israeli governments took steps towards privatization, liberalization in the foreign currency market and a reduction in the tax burden. Yet, along with the tremendous progress made by the state in various fields since its establishment, the social inequality has expanded to frightening proportions.

The Gini index is a measure or a coefficient for the inequality of the distribution of incomes. It is a number between 0 and 1 in which the coefficient of 0 means complete equality, meaning everyone has the same income, whereas the coefficient of 1 means total inequality, that is that one person has all of the income and the rest of the people have no income at all. According to this index, between 1998 and 2012, the inequality in Israel grew from 0.36 to 0.39 (in terms of gross economic income before transfer payments), which ranks it at 70th in the world and sets it as one of the states with the greatest economic inequality amongst the Western countries.[16,17] The Bank of Israel report for 2013 shows that during that same period (2012-1998), the gaps between the economic income of the residents of the (socially weak) periphery and the residents of the (well-established) center of the country also expanded.[18] The data for 2014 teaches us that the incidence of poverty — the percent of the public whose income is below the poverty line — and the inequality indexes in Israel are higher in comparison to the average among developed countries.[19]

### TABLE 2

## The incidence of poverty
## and inequality indexes
*Israel vs. the average of the OECD countries*

| Index | Israel | OECD average |
|---|---|---|
| The incidence of poverty of all of the people | 22% | 10.9% |
| Gini Index of disposable income | 0.360% | 0.308% |

*Source: The Knesset — National Insurance report for 2014*

According to the National Social Security report for 2014, 22 percent of Israelis — more than 1.7 million people, of them 770,000 children — live in poverty. This is in comparison to 21.8 percent in 2013.[20] This report also indicates the gaps in the levels of the poor families between the well-established center and the socio-economically weak periphery: in the center it's 11.6 percent, in the north it's 30.2 percent and in the south it's 19.5 percent of the poor families. You can see that poverty rates in Israel are higher than poverty rates in the European Union countries, whether it's in the general level or within the groups in the population that are at risk of poverty: children, senior citizens and women. Something that especially stands out is the high rate of children at risk of poverty in Israel: 31 percent in 2014, as compared to an average of 13 percent among European Union countries.[21] The report by the United Nations International Children's

Emergency Fund (UNICEF) for 2015 determines that in absolute terms the Israeli children are the poorest and that 27.5 percent of children in Israel are in poverty. They are even poorer than children in Romania, Mexico, Chile, Bulgaria and Greece.[22]

# 2.

## THE GAPS IN WELFARE EXPENDITURES

Government assistance for the needy population is one of the prominent characteristics of success in eradicating poverty. This assistance includes, among other things, allowances that provide social security and various social services. However, during the middle of the 1980's, the rate of government support in Israel for the needy began to gradually decrease.[23] The widening of the social gaps and the reverberation felt by the public that it created, caused the government to establish a committee for the war on poverty, the Alalouf committee, in 2013. The committee's objective was to present a comprehensive, long-term plan to cope with the social gaps and poverty. The committee set ambitious goals for fighting poverty and wanted to decrease the number of poor families in Israel by 50 percent within a decade. For that purpose, the committee recommended a significant increase in welfare budgets and the establishment of a central headquarters for the concentration of the war on poverty.

In the first two years (2015-2016) after the submission of the committee's report, the addition to the budgets of the government offices intended for dealing with poverty stood at 434 million shekels and 1.9 billion shekels in adjustment, despite the committee's recommendation of an addition of 7.4 billion shekels. The main recommendation of the committee — concentration of the activities for the eradication of poverty through a central body, which will be established and branched on to one of the central government offices — had not yet been implemented, and there was great doubt whether it would be established in the near future.[24] Despite the enormous gaps in inequality and the high poverty indexes, it seems that these topics are at the bottom of the ladder of national priorities. Otherwise, it is impossible to understand why the percent of public welfare expenditure as part of Israel's GDP is one of the lowest in the world — this perpetuates and deepens these gaps and places Israel at the bottom of the table, together with countries like Turkey, Chile and Mexico.[25]

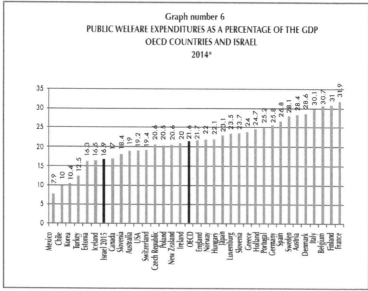

**Graph number 6**
**PUBLIC WELFARE EXPENDITURES AS A PERCENTAGE OF THE GDP**
**OECD COUNTRIES AND ISRAEL**
**2014***

Source: The OECD, the National Insurance, the Central Bureau of Statistics.
* Data for Chile, Turkey and New Zealand for 2013, data for Mexico for 2012, data for Japan for 2011.

The enormous gaps in education and the widening of social inequality that we've described support the widespread view recently held by Western countries and also by some sociologists in Israel: that social mobility, the ability to move from one socio-economic class to another, is most minimal, if not to say fictional. Social mobility is a characteristic of a society that has in it equal opportunity, meaning a society in which the odds for the individual to advance are not dependent on the individual's status or the status of his family. The economic historian, Gregory Clark, claims in his book The Son Also Rises that social mobility in the countries of the world today is no greater than it was in feudal England. The industrial revolution, the birth of the social state, public education and other social security networks that exist in any Western country today, liberal democracy and the rise in the quality of life that comes with it — all these things failed to improve the rate of social mobility beyond what was typical 200 or 300 years ago.[26]

Also, the gaps between the social classes are just getting wider. The wealth gaps between the classes are reaching a level of absurdity: in 2015, the world's top ten percent held 87.7 percent of the world's total wealth, and the highest percentiles held approximately 50 percent of that. In contrast, the five lowest deciles together hold less than one percent of the entire world's wealth.[27] Between 1979-2009, 36 percent of the increase in income of citizens of the United States flowed to the pockets of members of the top percentile.[28]

## The gap between the average incomes in the top quintile and the average incomes in the lowest quintile, according to the standard net income per person quintiles

|  | 2000 | 2002 | 2004 | 2006 | 2008 | 2010 |
|---|---|---|---|---|---|---|
| Sweden | - | 3.3 | 3.3 | 3.5 | 3.5 | 3.5 |
| Denmark | - | - | 3.4 | 3.4 | 3.6 | 4.4 |
| Finland | 3.3 | 3.7 | 3.5 | 3.6 | 3.8 | 3.6 |
| France | 4.2 | 3.9 | 4.2 | 4 | 4.2 | 4.5 |
| Austria | 3.4 | - | 3.8 | 3.7 | 3.7 | 3.7 |
| Belgium | 4.3 | - | 3.9 | 4.2 | 4.1 | 3.9 |
| Holland | 4.1 | 4 | 4 | 3.8 | 4 | 3.7 |
| Luxemburg | 3.7 | - | 3.9 | 4.2 | 4.1 | 4.1 |
| Ireland | 4.7 | - | 5 | 4.9 | 4.5 | 5.3 |
| Germany | 3.5 | - | 4.1 | 4.1 | 4.8 | 4.5 |
| Spain | 5.4 | 5.1 | 5.1 | 5.3 | 5.4 | 6.9 |
| Italy | 4.8 | - | 5.7 | 5.5 | 5.1 | 5.2 |
| UK | 5.2 | 5.5 | 5.6 | 5.4 | 5.6 | 5.4 |
| Greece | 5.8 | - | 5.9 | 6.1 | 5.9 | 5.6 |
| Portugal | 6.4 | 7.3 | 6.9 | 6.8 | 6.1 | 5.6 |
| EU Average | 4.5 | - | 4.8 | 4.6 | 4.9 | 5 |
| Israel | 6.5 | 7 | 7.6 | 7.4 | 7.5 | 8 |

*Source: Central Bureau of Statistics*

The Central Bureau of Statistics' Household Expenditure Survey for 2015 shows that in Israel, the income gap between the two highest deciles and the lowest two deciles rose from being 6.5 times greater in 2000 to 8.2 greater in 2015. This is the largest gap amongst the European Union countries. The net financial income of the two highest deciles in Israel constitutes 38.9 percent of the total income of households, compared with 6.4 percent in the two lowest deciles. The average monthly income for a household in the lowest decile in Israel in 2015 was 4,275 shekels, compared to 35,244 shekels per household in the highest decile. On the other hand, the monthly expenditure per household is 7,601 shekels in the lower decile, compared to 19,877 shekels in the upper decile.

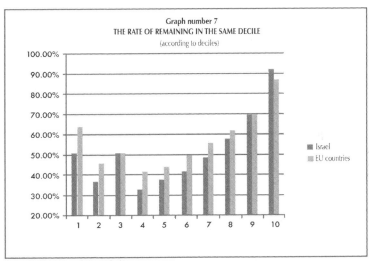

Source: Galit Ben Neim and Alexei Belinski

Also, in Israel, social mobility in the top three deciles is significantly lower than in the European Union. Between 1995 and 2009, an average of about 92 percent of the highest decile in a given year remained in the top decile the following year, compared with only 80.4 percent in the EU. In the lower decile, the level of social mobility in Israel is similar to that of EU countries. In the second, third and fourth deciles, the level of mobility in Israel is significantly higher than in the EU countries. However, a large proportion of those who succeeded to reach higher deciles rose only one decile. The prevalence of those who rose to one of the four highest deciles in Israel is lower than their prevalence in the European Union.[29]

# 3.

## SOCIAL MOBILITY THROUGH EDUCATION

"In every place in the world, the social mobility of the Jews is through education — except in the Jewish state," claims Prof. Moshe Halbertal.[30] The income gaps between the socio-economically weak periphery and the strong center and the weak educational system in the periphery make it difficult to create social mobility. Government funding of schools that do not teach core subjects (i.e., Math, English, etc.) actually strengthens the educational systems that inhibit social mobility. The degree of social mobility also influences the strength of the solidarity of Israeli society. If members of a particular group believe that their economic path is blocked or partially blocked, they are not expected to be sympathetic and will even develop hostility toward those they perceive as responsible for these barriers. This feeling is also important for the purpose of the Zionist project: the creation of a new nation from the ingathering of the exiles, in which some of whom sense a shared destiny as a people and disconnect from the tribalism that originated in the Diaspora.[31]

My individual case is an example of social mobility and the opportunities that are inherent in it. Yet, the social gaps that are just getting wider turn this example into an exceptional example that does not represent the whole.

Added to that is the fact that a significant portion of economists and sociologists claim that the social gaps and lack of social mobility that derives from them are a decree of fate — a claim that serves as an excuse for the inaction and helplessness of the state. Moreover, the fixation of this view also undermines the hope of members of the lower economic classes and serves as another artificial barrier to their dreams and aspirations of a better future.

The gaps between the parts of the State of Israel are also reflected in the health indicators and in the health services and their accessibility.[32] According to the World Health Organization measure, which is also used in Israel, gaps in education, income, culture and genetic characteristics (i.e. the marriage of relatives) also influence the health gaps. Inequality in the accessibility of health services and the difference in their quality and availability lead to large gaps in life expectancy, general mortality, infant mortality and an increased risk of serious diseases for the residents of the periphery relative to the residents of the center and of the poor in relation to the established middle class.[33]

The increase in inequality is a worldwide phenomenon. A report by the OECD summarizes the economic literature of its research on the topic in the world and presents the three main causes of the continuous increase in inequality: (1) technological improvements diverting human capital, which raises the productivity of the most highly educated individuals and not the productivity of the general population; (2) the processes of globalization, which are characterized by the fact that large and poor countries such as China and

India become a dominant factor in international trade and in setting the prices of products, especially products in developed countries that are produced by uneducated workers; and (3) weak regulation and the non-enforcement of labor laws that protect low-wage workers in the labor market.[34] These reasons can give some explanation for the level of the inequality in Israel but don't explain the fact that the levels of inequality in Israel and the pace at which they are expanding are among the highest in the Western world.

There are two populations that influence the high levels of poverty and inequality in Israel beyond their relative proportion in the population: the Arab sector and the ultra-Orthodox sector. These populations exist in parallel tracks to the Israeli mainstream and are largely cut off from it. According to the National Social Security report for 2015, the rate of poor Arab families rose from 47.4 percent in 2013 to 48.1 percent in 2014. The data in the report shows that 37.4 percent of the total poor people in Israel belong to this sector, while the portion of Arabs in the general Israeli population is just over 20 percent. While the portion of ultra-Orthodox in the general Israeli population is 9.6 percent, the portion of ultra-Orthodox families out of all of the poor families in Israel has reached 17.5 percent. The rate of poor ultra-Orthodox families rose from 52.1 percent in 2013 to 52.4 percent in 2014.[35]

The constant state of poverty in ultra-Orthodox society and the increase in the percentage of poor ultra-Orthodox families exist despite the positive trends in the rise in the number of ultra-Orthodox who joined the labor market.

In 2014, 48 percent of ultra-Orthodox men and 69 percent of ultra-Orthodox women were employed. This trend even improved in 2015, in which 52 percent of ultra-Orthodox men and 71 percent of ultra-Orthodox women were employed. The stubborn stance of the ultra-Orthodox leaders against military service and against core studies in ultra-Orthodox schools undoubtedly worsens their economic situation and condemns a large part of them to a life of poverty and deprivation and dependence almost entirely on the mercy of the state and the charity of others. Indeed, most of the responsibility falls on the state, which allows this situation in the first place and actually declares that it has no interest in the integration of the ultra-Orthodox sector into society.[36] Additionally, this situation leads to the formation of two states in Israel: the first is educated, with a bright future and high earning potential, and the other is poor, with no secure economic future and is dependent on the state that is next to it.[37]

Israel's small and limited geographical area, which leads to daily friction between the social extremes in Israel, heightens this visibility and illustrates the gaps in the eyes of the weaker socio-economic strata. Also, in a small country with mandatory military service, the immediate transition to civilian life at the end of the military service — while over the course of the military service there is this sense of equality that manifests between soldiers from all of the layers of society — causes the gaps to suddenly become apparent, and this transition becomes painful and frustrating. The social gaps and the deepening polarization between the population strata are destructive phenomena for society and cause severe damage to Israel's social resilience and solidarity. In the unique geo-strategic situation of the State of Israel, social resilience is vital to its national security.[38]

The social protest of the summer of 2011 brought to the surface the frustration that had been accumulating among hundreds of thousands of middle-class Israelis, and it gave expression to the sense of inequality among the many different sectors of the Israeli population. The main message of the protest touched on the inequality in society, on the asymmetry in bearing the burden and in the distribution of resources that harm the education system, employment and housing. This is despite the fact that the social inequality mostly effects the population from a low socio-economic background.[39] For most of the population in this socio-economic class, the preoccupation with the difficulties of making a daily livelihood consumes most of their time and energy, which doesn't allow them to be available for the fight and struggle for their rights. This weakness of the low socio-economic class is exploited by the various governments in decisions that undermine these groups and perpetuate their weakness. These are decisions that would not have passed quietly if they were aimed at strong populations.

One of these unfortunate decisions is in regard to the absorption of Ethiopian immigrants; there's no doubt that the absorption of Ethiopian immigrants in Israel has suffered from objective difficulties stemming from cultural differences and other factors. But the government made a tragic mistake in the way that they were absorbed and integrated into Israeli society. Instead of dispersing the immigrant population in relatively small groups to strong cities and communities that have the capability to cope with the special absorption difficulties of immigrants and provide the necessary infrastructure to support the gaps and lead to more rapid integration into society, the government referred the immigrants in large concentrations to a few weak development towns and housed them there — in what some would call "ghettos" — thus condemning both the weak veteran and immigrant population to poverty. The addition of the weak immigrant community from Ethiopia - which requires special means and resources for its absorption - to the communities of weak development towns has in any case seriously harmed both populations and has actually condemned them to prolonged suffering: the immigrants from Ethiopia did not receive the appropriate infrastructures, attention and support for their absorption, and the veteran population of the development towns was forced to compete with a new needy population for the already scarce resources.

Many strong cities and kibbutzes that are still living, as they claim, the Zionist ethos, basically did not at all join in on the absorption effort, to say the least. Many residents of the development towns saw the absorption of the immigrants as an important act of Zionism, which made it easier for the government and played into its hands, but the lack of awareness of the long-term implications for their wellbeing, as well as the daily hardships of making a living, prevented any opposition from the residents of the development towns toward the move. Such miserable decisions perpetuate the social gaps and increase poverty and inequality in Israel.

In order to correct, even if just a little bit, this malformation, many non-profit organizations (NGOs) and good people mobilized, contributed and invested a great deal of money and effort in setting up dozens of NGOs whose sole purpose is to create an improvement in the process of absorbing immigrants from Ethiopia. These NGOs are doing holy work, and many of them can be proud of their impressive achievements. Yet, the change, as important as it is, is a specific and limited change in the face of the enormous damage and severe repercussions of the government's decisions on the matter. The main role of these organizations is on two levels: on one hand, to repair malformations, which gives hope to the intended population and creates a sense of solidarity and caring, and on the other hand, to be like a stubborn and harassing mosquito in the ears of decision makers so that they will turn their attention to the issues.

Another example of bad government decisions that exploit the weak in society and have a significant impact on social gaps is the settlement of former Palestinian collaborators in neighborhoods of socio-economically weak populations. For example, in the poor neighborhood in Be'er Sheva where I grew up, most of the population consisted of immigrant families from North Africa, most of which are large families with many children and little financial capability. In the last few years (after the evacuation of the Gaza Strip), the state's institutions decided to transfer to this neighborhood several of the Palestinians who collaborated with the security forces in the struggle against their brethren. Almost every house in the neighborhood that became vacant was snatched by the Ministry of Defense and given to a Palestinian family. The transfer of the Palestinians to the neighborhood changed the social make-up that is in it, causing repeated frictions between the populations. Implementation of this decision created a great sense of frustration among the residents of the neighborhood, but the lack of social awareness and feelings of helplessness and inability to have an influence forced them to accept the malice of the decree.

This decree led to a decrease in the prices of the houses and apartments in the neighborhood, which were low as it was. The few that had the ability to, moved out of the neighborhood and the majority — the unable — having no other choice, remained in the neighborhood that they had lived in most of their lives and by then felt like strangers in it. The unbearable ease with which decisions with long-term social consequences are made while exploiting the helplessness of the weaker segments of the population is no less scandalous. What is happening, in reality, is they are providing an "easy" solution while creating bigger social problems at the expense of the weak and transparent. We can only imagine the uproar and resistance that would have broken out had the state tried to house these Palestinians in one of the established cities.

The gaps in education and the expansion of social inequality are social maladies shared by most developed Western countries. A healthy society that adopts a democratic-liberal-capitalist system of government consciously pays the price of reasonable social inequality. However, as we have seen, the enormous measures of social inequality in Israel are also exceptional in relation to the Western countries with similar methods of government. Despite these enormous gaps, the place of welfare problems in Israel in recent decades has sat at the bottom of the ladder of national priorities.

The huge gap in welfare expenditure between the average in European countries and Israel amounts to 4.7 percent of GDP (Graph 6 above). Meaning, in terms of 2015, this is approximately 70 billion shekels a year! This enormous gap inevitably leads to social gaps and to particularly high levels of inequality. Such absurd social gaps stem from, among other things, a national order of priorities that favors powerful and influential groups, aggressive economic policies, the absence of social safety nets for weaker populations and greedy, reckless, insatiable capitalist business conduct. Extreme social gaps are among the causes of the recent political polarization of government stability in part of the Western world. The radicalization and frustration of many citizens cause fundamental distrust of the government system. As a result, many of the citizens even see knowledge as an obstacle and a hindrance to solutions and are following astray after what Prof. Moshe Halbertal calls, "the charisma of ignorance" — charismatic, unknowledgeable leaders who offer magical solutions to complex situations. The gaps are a source of social instability, and they have the power to inflict upon us real social destruction.[40] The continued disregard of these gaps imposes the responsibility of the consequences on each and every one of us, as Albert Einstein claimed: "The world will not be destroyed by those who do evil, but by those who watch them without doing anything".[41]

# 4.

## NOT JUST THROUGH POLITICS

The sense of solidarity and a shared destiny is the glue of Israeli society. There are many among us who have high social awareness, who live the gaps and feel the pain of the situation. Evidence of this can be found in times of crisis and during the frequent wars, where the spirit of volunteerism soars and thrives in large parts of the nation. But in ordinary times, it is indifference that governs the lives of most of us with the feeling that there is nothing we can do to change the social situation. And out of this indifference, we all became accomplices to acts of injustice that are done in our name, as if they were a decree of fate. Apathy and indifference lead to insensitivity and encourage the state and its leaders to continue to ignore these gaps and their terrible implications for so many citizens. For many, the only way to influence is through political involvement. But political involvement requires compromises that "avert man from the truth as it is."[42] These are compromises that many of us do not want or are not able to make.

In addition, the negative impression that has been created in Israeli politics due to the corruption of a small portion of the politicians and a series of well-publicized trials in which a handful of ministers, a former president and a prime minister were convicted for corruption have led to feelings of disgust, disdain, and distrust of the politicians. These feelings were well expressed by Nobel Prize laureate S.Y. Agnon, who said, "*The sages wash their hands of world leadership because they know that there are wiser men than them and they want the world to be led by wise sages. All the while, fools and wicked men pounce and take the world into their hands and lead the world by their wickedness and stupidity.*"[43] It would be far from the truth and unfair to say that all of the politicians are corrupt. Israel is a unique and impressive story of success by any standard, and the different governments of Israel have done many good deeds and made great and important decisions in different areas that have advanced and strengthened Israel. The absolute majority of people who are in politics are honest, love the people and the country and have good will and intentions. Yet, as was said, in two important areas — education and social inequality — the results are an indication of severe and continuous failure.

It is important to mention that social gaps are not only a problem for the socio-economically weak layers of society but also for each one of us, for in a free society everyone bears responsibility.[44] Indeed, the main bearers of responsibility of the formation of the social gaps are the state and its institutions, yet our shared ownership of these institutions and the indifference and apathy that we display towards them turn us all into partners in this responsibility. Closing social gaps and reducing levels of inequality are among the main tasks of the state, but in many cases, the government's priorities are determined according to political constraints and pressures of powerful and influential interest groups that do not necessarily coincide with the needed priorities. Strong groups with political awareness and political connections will always have a great influence on setting priorities that benefit them. On the other hand, the weaker groups in society that are lacking political awareness have little or no influence on national priorities. In addition, the nature of government processes involving bureaucracy is cumbersome and managed very slowly. The government and the public sector are not designed to adopt and implement innovation in problem-solving unless they have already been tried and proved in other places. Also, as the representative executive branch of the people, the government is supposed to address the problems and needs that are common to broad segments of the population, and sometimes the special needs of small and weak groups remain unanswered. In recent years, there has been an increase in the number of non-profit organizations and associations in Israel, and the public interest in them has expanded. Some of the causes of this are the citizen's lack of confidence in the government's welfare policies and the increased power and influence of social movements. The "welfare state crisis" and the process of privatizing public services, a process that began in the 1980's and greatly developed in the 1990's, led to the establishment of thousands of new NGOs and the growth in the scope of activity of existing non-profit organizations. In many cases, the organizations provide complementary services or services as a replacement for what was previously provided by the state. Even before the privatization of public services, non-profit organizations played an important and central role. However, in the past two decades, a process has begun whereby the government has been transferring responsibility to private parties at its own initiative. The rationale of this is that private entities apparently have greater effectiveness. There is also the belief that they can obtain funds from additional sources.[45]

On the backdrop of the state dismantling from its social responsibility and the reduction of its support for public welfare expenditures and its social involvement, there is increasing importance of social involvement and solidarity in everything regarding building a proper, moral and just society. Clearly this social involvement cannot take the place of the government, and it does not clear the state of its responsibility. Moreover, the impact of social involvement — however high it may be — will always be significantly smaller than the state's power and budget and cannot replace the state in closing social gaps and providing solutions to national problems. However, social involvement is of great importance, and its impact and specific weight is greater than its total scope.

The extent of the social involvement of the citizens is first and foremost a testimony of the health, resilience and lack of indifference in the society. Beyond the social consequences of the social action itself, through social involvement, we state our commitment to society, express our dissatisfaction with national priorities and our lack of indifference to social gaps and inequality. In a society with high social involvement, that is caring and not indifferent — a society in which the cry for equality is not just heard from the throats of the weak — the social gaps will be intolerable. Such a society will also lead to moral, ethical and just solutions to be at the top of the national priorities.

Social involvement is to a great extent the conscience and compass of society. It is an expression of our lack of indifference and our discontent with the social injustices caused in our name by state institutions. It comes to soften, emphasize, correct distortions and defects, direct and complete the state's activity. To join in the effort, to raise public awareness of injustice, to propose new solutions and to push the government to adopt them. The strength of a society is measured by the way it relates to the weak and needy within it. A society that does not act for its own sake, a society without social solidarity and mutual responsibility, a competitive and aggressive society in which everyone cares only for himself and has no compassion for the weak is an impermeable society that has lost the basis of its human existence and is endangering its own stability. Such a society is an ill society that does not hear or see the sights, or in the striking words of Yaakov Rotblit:[46]

*And who will sing the song of the beggars,*
*the song of those abandoned at the side of the road*
*who also have a name and a face*
*and not just a back for doing hard labor,*
*the song of the laborer who can't really earn or save,*
*the downtrodden and hunched,*
*the song of the poor and the humiliated and the abandoned*

*who get their bread in soup kitchens?*
*And who will call out and say that this is very bad?*
*When did we learn to not hear, to not see*
*and to easily walk by the sights?*

In light of this, what remains for each one of us to do? Are we able to wash our hands clean and to ignore the social gaps as if they have nothing to do with us? Should we give up and accept the injustice and the enormous social gaps as just a matter of fate? On a moral level, can we just sit idle and watch from the side how, right before our eyes, social gaps emerge that condemn entire generations to poverty and deprivation? Is politics, which most of us cannot or do not want to pay the price for, the only way to influence and create change? Is knowing that we can change the world of even one child, of one adolescent, of one elderly person, of one Holocaust survivor — is that not enough to stir us into social involvement? Have we lost our compassion?

The values of compassion and kindness are the highest and most noble expressions of humanity, and they form a healthy, ethical, solid and compassionate society.[47] According to the Dahli Lama, true compassion is not just an emotional response but "a firm commitment founded on reason."[48] Human kindness is a value in human culture and is exclusive to human beings. The essence of kindness is a loving personal relationship with others, a bond that can enrich and sharpen the unique self of the parties involved and give meaning to their lives.[49] Solidarity focuses on local help that stems from a sense of compassion and identification. Even in a world based on pure egoism, egoism is not limited to the individual's survival, but it's also, and sometimes mainly, for the welfare of human society. In order for human society to survive, as its survivability also increases the chances of the individual to survive, individuals in society must give up some of their selfish qualities for the common good.[50]

Compassion, charity, kindness and concern for the weak are among the cornerstones of Jewish tradition. In this context, Rabbi Avraham Yehoshua Heschel wrote, "The essence of a Jew is his involvement in the plight of others, as God is involved. The secret of our tradition is that God is in every human situation and man must be involved in it... According to our tradition, anyone who forgets one passage from the Torah performs a great sin. How great is his guilt if he remains apathetic to the sorrow of one person?"[51] According to Rabbi Heschel, a Jew is not a specification of a person's ethnic belonging, rather "he is a person who is not indifferent to the suffering of others," therefore, as far as he is concerned, "Worship without compassion is worse than self-deception; it is an abomination,"[52] and Robert Ingersoll adds: "The hands that help are holier than the lips that pray."

Jewish tradition often deals with the commandments that are between one person and another and emphasizes them more than the commandments that are between man and God. This is why one of the more important rules in Judaism is: "Proper behavior precedes the Torah." There are many commandments in the Torah on assistance that are backed by the spirit of the prophets that call out, "It is to share your bread with the hungry, and to take the wretched

poor into your home; when you see the naked, to clothe him."
(Isaiah 58.7) These are the basic qualities of social solidarity.
In Jewish tradition, the utopian economy is not a socialist
economy in which absolute equality exists, and a capitalist
policy does not contradict Judaism.

The Torah of Israel does not object to financial
wellbeing, it even supports it. And it doesn't prohibit a
person from improving the quality of his life.[53] The Torah
allows a person to accumulate personal property, to trade
and make profits from his own money, and it does not expect
absolute economic equality and the abolition of economic
gaps in society. Those in need of support are a fact that exists
in society, as it is determined in the Torah: "For there will
never cease to be needy ones in your land." (Deuteronomy
15.11) Actually, a capitalist policy, in which there are also
class differences, is what enables a person to carry out his
desire to do charity and acts of kindness. However, alongside
the free economy, there is also a need for welfare policy. The
duty of charity that is imposed on the individual, "open your
hand to the poor and the needy kinsman in your land," does
not release the state from its responsibilities to care for the
weak.[54] The individual's duty and opportunity to care for the
weak does not come as a substitute for the general welfare
system but rather as a supplementary and softening addition.
This addition is the compassionate, caring and caressing
personal touch.

The fulfillment of the individual's opportunity to care for
the weak and to build a just society is done mainly through
Chessed (charity). Maimonides counts eight different

degrees of Chessed in descending hierarchical order. The highest level of Chessed, according to the Maimonides, is to help the poor or the weak, "in order to strengthen his hand until he need no longer be dependent upon others." Meaning, the aspiration is to give him a "fishing rod" and to teach him to "fish" independently so that he can get out of the cycle of poverty. The lowest level of Chessed, according to Maimonides, is to "give to him sorrowfully," meaning to give charity — or to give fish — from a place of having no other choice or out of compulsion.[55] Here, too lies the hope that the giver — even without a choice — will feel the positive energies and the ripples of the effect of his act of giving, and then the need and desire to climb up the "ladder of Chessed" will awaken in him, for "He who strives to do good and kind deeds attains life, success and honor." (Proverbs 21.21)

According to Jewish tradition, the act of Chessed is one of the main means for fulfilling the concept of Tikkun Olam (repairing the world), which expresses the desire to make the world a better and more just place. The ninth president of the State of Israel, Shimon Peres, defined the concept of Tikkun Olam like this: "What is the Jewish people's greatest contribution to the rest of the world? I would say that it is a lack of satisfaction. A real Jew cannot truly be satisfied. The moment he is satisfied, he begins to doubt his Judaism. A Jew is never satisfied... not with himself and not with others... Generation after generation, the Jewish people stood at the forefront of changes, thought and revolutions. Why? Because we do not sleep, we are in constant search, constantly thinking about something new, something different. Something that we call Tikkun Olam."[56]

Tikkun Olam is not done through revolutions or large and grandiose acts but through small, modest steps and perseverance. For helping to repair the world of one person is a reparation of an entire world. Each one of us is capable through our actions — even the smallest of them — of repairing the world. Maimonides went even further and determined: "If he were to fulfill just one mitzvah he would incline himself and the entire world toward merit and bring about salvation and redemption."[57] Exactly as Prof. Bergman's act of Tikkun Olam changed my world and indirectly changed the world of others from one end to the other.

The role of the act of giving is enormous, and it has the ability to make a significant and transformative change. The act of giving actually has a life of its own. Giving is personal; it enriches and, to a large extent, it also shapes the heritage and identity of the giver. It also leads to a balanced order of priorities, courtesy and modesty. The ripples of impact and implications of the act are beyond the intention of the giver. They change worlds and bring out the good and the beauty in people. Giving actually has immediate and long-term benefits. These actions fill us at the time of the act and also leave us with a sense of meaning and purpose over time. Acts of giving are the only things that are truly ours forever. They become part of our identity. We can lose everything, but what we have given to the world will always be ours. The inspiration, the satisfaction, the balance and the meaning achieved through giving are unique, and no other sense of success can be compared to them.

In many ways, the inspiration and feeling of transcendence of the experience of giving is similar to the cosmic religious feeling underlying scientific research, as Einstein described it: "I think that we are all familiar with this feeling to a certain extent, even if it is hard for us to remember it: it is the same excitement that fills us when we are surprised to see a beautiful landscape before us or are witnesses to a gesture of generosity or goodness on the part of someone, or give up from a place of true wholeness on something that 'we deserve.'"[58]

For most people in the world, achieving happiness is one of the main aspirations. Yet, despite the clear and strong desire for personal happiness, the path to achieving it is unclear. One of the reasons for this lack of clarity is that even though people think they know what it is that will lead them to happiness, their expectations around what will make them happy are sometimes inaccurate. To a great extent, the more we are occupied with our own happiness, the more it slips away from us, and in fact only when we are occupied with someone else — from a real and pure place — we can truly touch happiness.

It's no wonder that many studies have shown that social involvement for the sake of others intensifies a person's sense of inner well-being and happiness.[59] This fact is even supported by the findings in the Central Bureau of Statistics' Social Survey of 2013 that determined that "people who engage in volunteer activities are more satisfied with their lives and more optimistic about their future than people who do not engage in volunteer activities."[60] Another significantly important "profit" gained from being occupied with Tikkun Olam is meeting good and wonderful people. People with a common value base constitutes the basis for true friendships.

I do not want to sound like a preacher. I understand that we are all occupied with the difficulties of making a living, our routine and our daily lives. But one of our challenges in life is to find the right balance between being enslaved to daily life, material needs and dealing with ourselves — and the ability to lift our heads to see, hear and respond to the needs of the other. This challenge is not new, but it is more relevant than ever. Already, 2,500 years ago, the Greek philosopher Socrates presented it the people of Athens:[61] "*Best of men... from the city that is greatest and best reputed for wisdom and strength: are you not ashamed that you care for having as much money as possible, and reputation, and honor, but that you neither care for nor give thought to prudence, and truth, and how your soul will be the best possible?... For I go around and do nothing but persuade you, both younger and older, not to care for bodies and money before, nor as vehemently as, how your soul will be the best possible I say: Not from money does virtue come, but from virtue comes money and all of the other good things for human beings both privately and publicly.*"

Our concern and help for each other, help that comes from within us and for us, and for the weak and needy among us, is the ultimate eternal goodness. For the philosopher Emmanuel Levinas, the good is not an abstract concept or an idea. On the contrary, "the good is involved in social relationships, in real gestures that express our concern for others and respect for otherness."[62] Each of us has a choice between two fundamentally different ways of life: ignoring the distress of others, focusing on ourselves, surrendering and giving in to our natural inclinations is one possibility. This way requires no effort, it is the way of a rock rolling down a slope.

The other way of life is a bit more difficult, and it is that of social involvement — the path of philanthropy, which means love of humanity, love of others. Love, according to Levinas, is an "insatiable hunger. Shaking a friend's hand is meant to express friendship towards him, but also to express something that is impossible to express, something that is unending, like constant desire."[63] The people who choose to give are caring, involved, loving people. The Danish philosopher, Soren Kierkegaard, believed that eternity would ask all of us only one question: "Did you live your life from despair or from love?"[64]

# CHAPTER THREE:

# MOTIVES FOR SOCIAL ACTION AND SOCIAL INVOLVEMENT

*He who has a why to live can bear almost any how.*

- Friedrich Nietzsche

# 1.

## THE SIGNIFICANCE OF THE MOTIVE FOR SUCCESS

Albert Einstein claimed that "feeling and longing are the motive force behind all human endeavor and human creation."[1] This claim is also true regarding social involvement. Each journey of Tikkun Olam is always driven by a strong desire to change something. The source of the desire is different from one case to another, but the sense of inner commitment and passion for the specific subject that we wish to promote are essential to the success of the journey. This journey is also a journey of self-discovery, a journey into our inner selves to find out who we really are. To a large extent, our journey of giving also defines us, and the path molds and shapes the essence and identity of the person who walks it. But, like any journey, this journey also requires careful preparation in order to increase the chances of its success. Before embarking on this journey, the first question we must clarify for ourselves in an honest and true way is: What is our motive for embarking on the journey? A strong, deep and true motive is critical — yet not enough — for success in the social journey. The motive must be a sense of inner commitment, something that burns in our bones, for which we are prepared to sacrifice the best of our energy and resources. A good motive is a sort of autopilot that pushes, lifts and urges us through the many anticipated moments of crisis that await us on this journey.

The seed of my social journey was already planted in my first encounter with Prof. Bergman. The seed sprouted and grew into a strong motive and tremendous personal commitment to give back to society and to continue the influence of the good deed that was done with me. After completing my master's degree, I decided to continue on for a doctorate. I, of course, consulted with Prof. Bergman, and he recommended that I study in the United States. And so, in 1987, I went to the United States to study. I then went into business in software development. After more than 13 years in the US, I returned to Israel; but during my 13 years there, I did not stop thinking about the implications of my meeting with Prof. Bergman. I very much wanted to understand what it was in that encounter that so fundamentally affected me, and how to explain my case and that of others who shattered the statistics and succeeded against all odds. How is it that my four older and talented siblings fell in this statistical framework, whereas I and all my younger siblings deviated from and evaded the terrible statistics in every parameter?

I am convinced that had my older siblings been given the opportunity to study, as I was given, they would have achieved advanced degrees and would have fully materialized their tremendous potential. But, the economic reality that led them to abandon their studies in order to help support the family cut off this possibility. On the other hand, the fact that I studied at the university shattered artificial barriers for my younger siblings and changed their awareness, making academic studies something real, accessible and possible for them. Thus, in the end, all of my younger siblings completed advanced degrees in academic institutions. This fact proves beyond any doubt that the potential lies in everyone, to some degree or another, but the odds of actualizing the potential depends on external circumstances, mainly social and economic. True, academic studies are not the most important thing and do not guarantee success, but an academic degree significantly increases the chances of materializing personal potential, integrating into advanced society, social mobility and economic success.

I'm not denying the low chances of success that come with the difficult starting point and obstacles faced by those of the low socio-economic class. I'm also not denying that not all people have the same abilities and talents. But I do strongly object to the assertion by some of the researchers that this is a decree of fate and that there is nothing we can do to change it. Can we deny the fact that there are many children with abilities and potential who are not given the opportunity to express and actualize it? As many studies have confirmed, the chance of success in life does not require special talent. The truly important characteristics of success are the desire to work hard, the willingness to invest, the ability to overcome failures and delay gratification.[2] These traits are present and even intensified in children and adolescents who grow up in a state of deprivation. But, in order to implement them, they must first be given the opportunity to remove the artificial barriers and to believe in themselves.

The empowering experience I had during my childhood

as a result of the encounter with Prof. Bergman and the tremendous implications of his good deed — on my life and indirectly on the lives of my younger siblings — placed a huge responsibility on me to pass on the message and continue to intensify the impact of his deed. My motive was the strong desire to play the same role in the lives of children and youth from backgrounds similar to mine. This desire led me to my social journey — to my own personal Tikkun Olam — the establishment of Ofanim, an organization for the advancement of children and youth in Israel. From many years of experience working with children and youth and from the experience of many other good people, I know that through social action we are able to influence, change and improve, even if it is just slightly, the reality of our lives and the lives of others. Social action, even the smallest bit, can strike waves and reverberate at a distance with great force.

There is a wide variety of motives for social action and involvement in Israel. The main motives are collective responsibility and patriotic identification, a sense of belonging to a community and a desire to give back to the society in which the giver is part of and owes his success to. Other reasons include the search for meaning and for internal gratification, a change in life circumstances or a life-altering event, a desire to promote certain issues, the pressure of colleagues in the social or business environment, taxation and business positioning.[3] Sometimes the motive for giving is paradoxical and multidimensional. It can stem at the same time from both constraints and from utilitarianism but also from a place devoid of interests. The act of giving is a social act loaded with meaning, and its results exceed the boundaries of the original motive.[4] Whatever the reason for giving and involvement may be, all giving and social involvement stemming from a true and pure motive are welcomed with a blessing. In many cases, passive support for social action leads to active involvement and sometimes becomes a way of life and positively affects many people. Doing something at first not for its own sake, can eventually turn into doing it for its own sake.

# 2.

## THE POWER OF MOTIVE

"It is [easy] to give and spend money," claimed Aristotle, "but to... give money to the right person, and in the right amount, and at the right time, and for the right purpose, and in the right way—this is not within everybody's power, and is not easy."[5] It is important that our motive for social involvement be the right motive, a motive that comes from a true and pure place. Many good social entrepreneurs in Israel invest their time, energy and money to create amazing social enterprises, and it is hard to imagine Israeli society without them. There are social initiatives that have changed the face of society in Israel for the better and are a testimony to the good, beautiful and humane side of it. Common to all, as the following examples demonstrate, is the tremendous personal commitment and the pure and true motive.

Ran Naor, a young man, had his own rhythm in life. A rhythm that swept family and friends away with him, but sometimes they did not keep the pace that Ron dictated, and they slowed down and watched in wonder as he moved on, wanting more and more. Despite his fast pace, Ran would occasionally slow down, take a look around, raise substantial questions and wonder about life and the world, and his friends knew that it was possible to have deep conversations with him into the late night hours. Before his enlistment in the IDF, Ran managed to travel with his friends on a trip full of experiences in Europe, and then he traveled with his parents and girlfriend, Dana, in the United States.

One of Ran's great loves was his jeep, which he liked to drive on the sand of the beach accompanied by his friends. On June 12, 1995, when Ran was 19 years old, he went on break from the army to complete a matriculation exam. After the exam, Ran took his jeep out for a ride on Mandarin Beach in Herzliya. During the ride, the jeep flipped over and Ran was killed. After he died, his commander described him like this: "You were a lively kid, Ran. I would look at you, your handsomeness, your powerful uprightness, abundant with goodness and joy, and say to myself, what a wonderful kid he is, the salt of the earth... I found in you, Ran, so many contradictions, side by side. Such complexity that I don't remember finding before, not within myself, not even within other young people your age."

Ran was the son of one of the leading business people and philanthropists in Israel, winner of the Israel Prize for Lifetime Achievement & Special Contribution to Society and the State in 2014, Avi (Avinoam) Naor. Immediately after the tragedy, the Naor family set up a monument to commemorate Ran, and the initial thought was to establish a non-profit organization with a view that was limited to the context of the son who was killed. The struggle against road accidents began to preoccupy Avi, and he embarked on an in-depth exploration of the subject. He gradually came to understand that Israel's situation in the area of road accidents was very difficult in comparison with other countries, especially with countries that had made reforms in the matter. This understanding led him to recognize that he must move from emotional and personal aspects to the rational aspect and make the struggle against road accidents into a national struggle. Avi was determined to harness the state to carry out a fundamental reform in the matter, and he decided to dedicate the best of his time, energy, experience and resources for that purpose. In 1997, the organization Or Yarok was established with the declared objective of minimizing the number of casualties caused by road accidents as much as possible and to influence change in the driving culture in Israel.

According to Avi's view, the role of social entrepreneurship is to raise awareness of the overall social issue that is close to the heart of the entrepreneur and to harness the state to promote it. "A country can build infrastructure, but cannot change the patterns of thinking of the public," he says. In his opinion, the power of civil society is greater than that of politics, especially when the public is mobilized for a cause. A government minister, in his view, promotes the affairs of his ministry with the recognition that the average length of a minister's service is less than two years, and therefore he cannot apply deep reforms for change and deep promotion of the issues of his ministry. The desire that the achievements of a given ministry will be attributed to the minister who heads it and that they will be expressed during his tenure, causes many ministers to change the plans and decisions of their predecessors and to even cancel them and promote short-term programs instead. A minister does not have a proper amount of time during his tenure to study in depth the endeavor and its implementation. It is into this void that programs of civil society enter. Non-profit organizations have the ability to formulate in-depth programs, to start running them as a pilot, to encourage the government to join the success of these programs, and be a gatekeeper whose existence extends beyond the tenure of a minister or of a government.

In order to raise social awareness of the war on road accidents, Or Yarok decided to establish the "Caesarea Road Safety Conference," which is held annually. Over the years, prime ministers, government ministers, social workers, journalists and experts from around the world have attended the conference. The purpose of the conference was to make the state recognize its responsibility for road safety and not to place responsibility for accidents only on drivers and to significantly increase the budget for road safety — investment in infrastructure, deepening public education and acceptance of responsibility for changing national behavior. For this purpose, the organization published a series of position papers clarifying that only a multi-disciplinary, multi-year national plan could give a "root-canal" treatment in road accidents and cut the number of fatalities and casualties in half.

For many, this goal seemed excessive and even charlatan, but Avi and the organization were determined to lead the government to adopt the plan. Indeed, in 2003 the Israeli government, headed by Arik Sharon, decided to adopt the multi-year national program for the war on road accidents, which was led by a committee headed by Dr. Yaakov Sheinin and supported by "Or Yarok." The adoption of the program led to a positive change in the awareness and driving culture in Israel and a decrease in the number of road accident casualties. In 2003, before the plan was accepted, there were 445 fatalities and 2,416 serious injuries in Israel, compared to 378 fatalities and 1,909 serious injuries in 2016.[6] "I believe that my whole life and my entire career were preparation for my activity in "Or Yarok," Avi concluded. Thus, what began as a personal-emotional initiative to commemorate his son Ran became Avi's life's mission and a national program that many Israeli citizens owe their lives to.

A strong desire for Tikkun Olam and a sense of moral social commitment do not require capital or superhuman efforts to turn an idea into action. Theodore Roosevelt, the 26th president of the United States, said, "Do what you can, with what you have, where you are." Social involvement can be in different capacities: from supporting the community in which we live through a limited contribution of time or resources in an organization that promotes a goal that is close to our heart to the decision to establish a new organization dedicating our best efforts, energy and resources to advance an interest that is dear to us. The decision to establish a new organization is not a simple one. It requires an understanding of the total commitment and ongoing efforts involved in it. The establishment of a new organization is a long, difficult and sometimes exhausting journey. It is a unique journey that contains many different challenges. It has its ups and downs and high and low moments. But, this is a journey in which the real sacrifice creates touches of grace, giving and reaching out to others. This is a journey in which every step fills our hearts with so much satisfaction, pride and meaning that it's doubtful whether one can feel anything like it from any kind of success in business. To a certain extent, this journey also defines us, becomes part of our identity and brings out the best of us and the beauty that is in us. Beyond the tremendous satisfaction and meaning, the greatest privilege that persists over time in this journey is meeting good people who walk with us along the way and the true friendships that may emerge from this acquaintance.

The preparation for Judith Recanati's social journey already began during her childhood. She absorbed the connection to the land and the nation in the warm Jewish-Israeli home where she grew up and in the Scout movement in which she spent most of her time. She received the values of giving and helping others from her parents and especially from the legacy of her grandfather, Leon Yehuda Recanati, the head of the Jewish community in Salonika and an active and energetic social activist for the Sephardic community in Israel. The values and connection to the people and the heritage that she absorbed in her home led her, after serving as an officer in the IDF, to study archeology. "Because I wanted to strengthen my connection to my history and my past," she explained. But the Yom Kippur War, which was a major breaking point for her, interrupted her plans. The physical and mental injuries sustained by many of her friends and neighbors deeply affected her. Her anxiety and concern increased during the war because Israel, who she married immediately after the war, was serving in the reserves.

Judith's parents passed away when she was 33 years old. As a result, she decided to study art therapy for adults and specialized in treating trauma victims. Despite having been surrounded by abundance during her childhood, Judith turned to doing hard work at Tel Hashomer Hospital and Beit Levinstein Hospital. "There I understood that even after trauma and loss of life, there is a way to help people come back to life. A life that is different, but meaningful," she said. In addition to her work within these frameworks, Judith studied psychotherapy at Bar Ilan University, where she met her professional guide, Dr. Yossi Hadar, who was the head of the Elie Wiesel Holocaust Post Trauma Institute. This encounter left a deep impression on her and was a formative "key experience" for her. Judith understood that her mission was to help trauma victims, but she still did not know how to fully express it.

During the Yom Kippur War, Dr. Hadar's battalion almost fell captive to the Syrians in the Golan Heights, and he saw and felt the terrible consequences of the war in the eyes of his shell-shocked soldiers. Similar to them, there were also many others who returned from the war in a not so simple mental condition. In those days, Israeli society did not know how to contain the trauma, and the many victims did not have an address to turn to. Dr. Hadar knew about Judith's strong emotional attachment to trauma victims and the paramount importance that she saw in treating these victims. In 1997, he told her about his dream of establishing an organization that would treat post-trauma victims of terrorism, military service and wars. Judith enthusiastically responded to Dr. Hadar's request, and they began the preparations for the establishment of the organization NATAL — the Israel Trauma Center for Victims of Terror and War — from a desire to bring to public awareness the fact that Israeli society must recognize that there are many people within it that are in need of psychological guidance and assistance. Thus, in June of 1998, NATAL was officially established. About a month after that, Dr. Yossi Hadar was diagnosed with leukemia, and he died two weeks later. "I felt a tremendous commitment to the last will of Dr. Hadar *z"l*, a commitment that came out of identification with the idea and the need, a commitment that became the purpose of life for me," she added. The purpose of the life spoken of by Judith is to raise awareness and provide an answer and address for the many people who suffer from post-traumatic stress disorder, which amounts to approximately 15 percent of the citizens in Israel.

"NATAL was founded from the vision and dream of Yossi z"l, who passed the scepter to me. He was a man of spirit and vision, and I turned his will into a present and influential reality. The connection between us was the hand of fate that allowed it to happen," Judith concludes. Thanks to the culture of business and organizations that she absorbed from her family, Judith has transformed NATAL into one of the world's leading organizations in this field. The organization distributes the knowledge and great experience it has accumulated to various organizations around the world. In Israel, NATAL has handled more than 210,000 people to date and has become the main and only address focusing on trauma victims on a national background. Indeed, it is hard to imagine Israel, a country that has the experience of wars and terror attacks, without NATAL. It would not be an exaggeration to say that tens of thousands of people owe their sanity and mental health to this organization.

One of the motives for social involvement is a change in life circumstances or a life-altering event. A difficult and unfortunate event led Yuval Wagner to establish one of the most important non-profit organizations in Israel to promote accessibility for people with disabilities, with the purpose of allowing them a normal life. On March 18, 1987, when he was 20 years old, Yuval Wagner flew a Cobra fighter helicopter of the 160 Squadron, which crashed due to a technical malfunction. Yuval miraculously survived the crashed, but was left as a disabled person — paralyzed from the shoulders down, subject to the permanent use of a wheelchair. Since he was the son of a disabled IDF veteran, who also used a wheelchair, he was already familiar with the topic of disability and accessibility, which helped him through his rehabilitation. Despite his handicap, Yuval remained in career military service and even attained the rank of lieutenant colonel in the Israeli Air Force. During his new life in a wheelchair, Yuval encountered an unbearable situation in which he wanted to reach many places, but these places were not accessible to him. He wrote a letter to the president of Israel at the time, Ezer Weizman, in which he complained that he could not educate his children in the important value of patriotism because Israel is so inaccessible to the disabled. In response to his letter, the president proposed to Yuval that he establish an organization that would promote the topic of accessibility in Israel. Yuval took on the challenge and established the organization Access Israel, which promotes accessibility and integration to improve the quality of life of the 1.6 million disabled people and their families who live in Israel.

The absolute belief in the importance of the topic and the basic necessity of his own life motivated Yuval to completely devote himself to this enterprise. In his opinion, the state should have assumed the role, but because it did not, "the alternative of not doing anything is not an option," he said. "The government has neither knowledge nor innovation. The role of philanthropy is to change reality, to change the method, and to force the system to contribute its share." As of today, after 18 years of extensive activity, thanks to the activities of Access Israel, Israel has become one of the leading and most advanced countries in the area of accessibility for the disabled. In July 2016, Access Israel was awarded the status of special advisor to the UN Economic and Social Council (ECOSOC), thereby receiving recognition for its role as a global leader in the field. This council is the main forum for the formulation of recommendations to the UN and its member states in the area of economic and social policy.

Yuval, who serves as the president of the organization, is the one who outlines the vision, initiates innovative work, challenges the organization and brings new energy to it. Recently, he even set a new goal for the organization: to turn

Israel into a technologically accessible country, one that will be a world leader in all that is connected to digital service, smart cities and the like. "The destiny of my life led me to set up the accessibility enterprise," says Yuval. Thus, social involvement, which began as a result of a life-altering event, became "a life's mission and valuable and meaningful work."

Motives for social involvement stem from conscious and unconscious factors. Sometimes, only after deep involvement and hindsight can we explain to ourselves what the source of the tremendous energy that we derive from ourselves is and what our real motive for social action is. I have no doubt that the education that a person absorbs in his childhood home is a central component in the motives of many of the social entrepreneurs, and the best education is by personal example. An example of such an initiative is the establishment of Beit Issie Shapiro. Issie Shapiro z"l was a warm Jewish man from Johannesburg. One of Issie's good friends had a daughter who was born with complex disabilities. In those days, society's attitude toward such children was denial, repression and estrangement. Shapiro was very sensitive to his good friend's distress and began to take an interest in the subject and learn about it. He met many people along the way with a similar problem, but there was no solution present. He found that families of children with such disabilities each cope with the problem in their own way, so he decided to take action. He established in Kensington, a suburb of Johannesburg, a boarding school for children and adults with mental retardation called Selwyn Segal Hostel when his daughter Naomi turned eleven years old.

This act was burned and planted in the consciousness of Naomi Shapira, who later became Stuchiner, and sprouted decades later when she established Beit Issie Shapiro in her father's memory, which works to change the quality of life for disabled people and their families. This institution has marked 36 years of social change and influence on the lives of some 30,000 people each year in Israel and abroad. Beit Issie Shapiro has become the pre-camp pioneer in everything regarding the treatment, integration and improvement of the lives of disabled children and their families. In July 2012, the institute was recognized as a world leader in the development of innovative treatments for improving the quality of life of people with disabilities and, like the organization Access Israel, received the status of special advisor to the Economic and Social Council (ECOSOC). In addition to these organizations, there are 14 other Israeli organizations that have received this status.

"I had the privilege of growing up in a family where giving and helping others was a part of life. I was educated to fight for the rights of the weak and needy in society and to believe in our ability to cause change," Naomi says, and adds, "Education and the awareness of giving begins at an early age." Thus, the influence of Issie's sensitive social action on his daughter Naomi could be seen already at a young age. An act that began with her father's sensitivity and concern for his friend's distress constituted the foundation for the establishment of one of the most unique institutions in the world. What is the same in all of the motives of the entrepreneurs we presented is their complete inner commitment. For Avi Naor, the motive began as the desire to fight the war against his son Ran's unnecessary death, which became his life mission, a mission that turned into a national mission and saved the lives of many people in Israel. For Judith Recanati, the social values that she absorbed from her grandfather, Leon, matched the will of Dr. Yossi Hadar, a will that became her life mission. For Yuval Wagner, a fateful and unfortunate accident led to his life mission of taking action to make Israel more accessible and to improve the lives of tens of thousands of people with disabilities. And for Naomi Stuchiner, the education of giving that she received from a young age and the belief that she has the power to create change have led to a way of life that is entirely acting for the weak and needy.

For me, as I mentioned, it was the random encounter with Prof. Bergman. I remember how during my 13 years in the United States I never stopped thinking about this encounter and its implications. The thought that by generating empowering key experiences, we have the power to make a significant positive opening in the lives of children and adolescents who come from backgrounds and environments similar to my own captivated my imagination and gave me a tremendous sense of commitment. This sense never left me, and over the years, it became a sense of mission and led to the establishment of Ofanim. In retrospect, it can be said that the seed for the establishment of the organization was sown in 1974, in my first meeting with Prof. Bergman, and sprouted about 30 years later.

# 3.

## SOCIAL INVOLVEMENT IN ISRAEL

Social involvement in which citizens undertake initiatives to promote social issues that are important to them is a very important component in the development of a civil society. The strength and might of democratic societies are measured, amongst other things, by the involvement of their citizens. The extent of social involvement in Israel is usually related to times of national or personal crisis, and to a desire for social, economic or political change. In wartime, the spirit of volunteerism among the people skyrockets, and the shared fate minimizes that which separates and emphasizes that which unifies the people. Social initiatives and social entrepreneurs operate in the same spirit and intensity, both in times of crisis and during routine times. It is important to remember that social involvement is not the domain of particular or special people — social involvement is a way of life. Each person according to how he can serve, volunteer and give. Volunteering, helping and giving bring out the best in a person. Social involvement makes us more committed and caring citizens and connects us to the people and to the land. As I mentioned above, the preoccupation with and consideration of the needs of the other provides a perspective on the truly important things and brings real meaning to our lives. The mobilization of people, companies and organizations to create and support social initiatives is one of the hallmarks of a society that is not indifferent, and is connected, healthy and sensitive.

In conversations with people about social involvement, I often hear the excuse: "At the moment I am busy building myself and I cannot be available," or "When I finish the... I will be freed up for social involvement." Our sages said about this, "And do not say 'When I have time I will study' because you may never have the time."[7] Anyone who has experienced the pleasure, the satisfaction and the tremendous meaning of social involvement cannot understand how many others in Israeli society do not partake in it. Their lack of involvement mostly stems from the many various barriers. First of all, studies show that education for giving and for social involvement increases giving and social involvement, but in Israel, there is no set educational tradition to encourage giving and social involvement, and few people take it on. In addition, the negative image that has emerged for Israeli non-profit organizations distances many good people from philanthropy and social action. The acts of corruption in a small portion of the organizations that were publicly exposed and the headlines of exaggerated salaries of some of the NGO leaders created a negative image among broad sectors of the public and among potential donors.[8]

The antagonism that exists among the general public towards the wealthy, especially those who became wealthy through business in Israel, also leads to social giving being seen by a large portion of the public as a privilege of those with the means and as an act of self-interest. This negative impression does great injustice to the vast majority of those involved in social action and giving and deters many others from entering the field. In addition, during the first decades of its existence, Israel was run as a welfare state with socialist characteristics. This is why many people still expect the state to take care of all of the needs and see no room for social involvement of citizens. On the other hand, in recent decades we have become a society that sanctifies individualism and the self-fulfillment of the individual, and one that places particular emphasis on material values. In contemporary culture, "priority is given to externality, immediacy, visibility, superficiality and temporariness — what is real is rejected because of the impression."[9] Nevertheless, substantial social action is being carried out in Israel by quite a few committed and caring people who cannot remain indifferent to the enormous social gaps. Since the Non-profit Organizations Act was passed in Israel and took effect in 1981, more than 52,000 organizations have been registered according to this act, which of them approximately 40,000 registered in the Israeli Corporations Authority.[10] Approximately 32 percent of the organizations that were registered up to 2013, and in general, ceased to exist and were closed.[11] From the registered organizations, only about 15,000 have remained in operation.[12] This number includes public institutions, like hospitals, health clinics, institutions of higher education, etc. All of the organizations operate under The Amutot (Non-Profit Organizations) Law, 5740-1980 and are supervised by the Registrar of Non-Profit Organizations. The purpose of the Amutot Law is to establish standards and a code of conduct suitable for anyone wishing to operate under a corporation registered as a non-profit organization. In practice, despite the application of the Amutot Law in 1980, for almost a decade, it has hardly been used. Many non-profit organizations acted negligently, without holding meetings as required by the Amutot Law, and not submitting documents in a consistent and orderly fashion, thus the law had no validity or substantiality. In fact, up to 1995, registered non-profit organizations could receive large amounts of money without any control mechanism and supervision. The vast majority of the non-profit organizations do sacred work in all areas of life, but the widespread media response to the corruption of a small number of the associations has given them all a bad name.

Since 1995, there has been a gradual transformation in the world of non-profit organizations. The Amutot Law has been and continues to undergo many changes aimed at controlling and enforcing appropriate regulation on organizations. Today, the control and supervision of non-profit organizations is tighter, and only organizations that uphold the procedures set by the Registrar of Non-Profit Organizations receive the approval of "proper management." In addition, organizations seeking recognition by the Income Tax Authority as public institutions for donations under section 46 (equivalent to the 501C (3) in the US) are also more closely supervised by the Income Tax Authority itself. This is because the conditions for recognition of donations by the Income Tax Authority are added to the conditions required to obtain "proper management" approval from the Registrar of Organizations. An example of this can be seen in the different requirement for a minimum number of board members according to the instructions of the Registrar of Organizations, as opposed to the requirement to obtain income tax approval under section 46. Receiving recognition by the Income Tax Authority as a public institution for donations is essential for the purpose of raising funds from private donors, especially from institutions and public bodies. Beyond the recognition of the contribution itself, for the vast majority of donors, the recognition by the Income Tax Authority of an organization under Section 46 constitutes a sort of basic "kosher certificate." This is why less than 12 percent of registered organizations are recognized by the Income Tax Authority as a public institution for donations.

The total philanthropy of the GDP in Israel was 0.87 percent in 2014, compared to 2 percent in the United States. The main philanthropic objectives of non-profit organizations, both in Israel and in the United States, are in the fields of welfare, education, research and religion. At the same time, the main destinations of donations in Israel is non-profit organizations in the field of welfare: it is 39 percent in Israel, compared to 13 percent in the United States, while in the United States, the main target of donations is non-profit organizations in the field of religion: which is at 33 percent, compared to 15 percent in Israel.

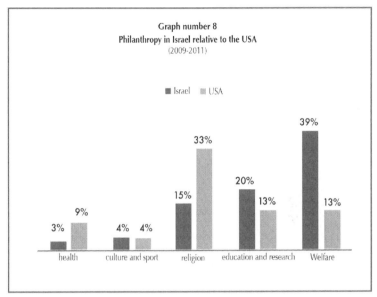

**Graph number 8**
**Philanthropy in Israel relative to the USA**
(2009-2011)

■ Israel   ■ USA

| | health | culture and sport | religion | education and research | Welfare |
|---|---|---|---|---|---|
| Israel | 3% | 4% | 15% | 20% | 39% |
| USA | 9% | 4% | 33% | 13% | 13% |

Source: Central Bureau of Statistics

There are thousands of non-profit organizations operating in various fields in Israel. Like any organization, non-profit organizations also encounter difficulties and crises throughout their years of activity. Unlike companies and for-profit organizations, whose main measure of success is the profit index, the main distinction between successful and unsuccessful organizations is the strength of their people's motivation and commitment. The existence of a leadership with a spark in its eyes, which regards the goals of the organization as its life mission, is vital to the success of the organization in achieving its objectives. This is especially true during the critical stages of the organization's life — the first two or three years. Therefore, a leadership that recognizes and identifies with the organization's goals and is committed to its success is required. A leadership that will spare no effort to initiate, push and promote the goals of the organization. A leadership that will be the spirit and the anchor, and will be the backbone of the organization. For the most part, the strength of the devotion and faith of the leadership spreads to the other members of the organization, the target audience, the donors and the supporters. When these people raise a flag that conveys commitment and credibility, devotion and integrity — others gather under it. These people are the "extra soul" of the organization. The chances of success of non-profit organizations to survive and to achieve their goals are significantly higher when they have "extra souls."

# 4.

## OFANIM — GETTING STARTED

From a deep analysis and observation of my experience with Prof. Bergman, I understood that the environment in which a child is raised — the home, the friends, the school, the residential neighborhood, etc. — shapes his life and to a large extent determines the boundaries of his future. A limited environment, which instills in the child feelings and experiences of failure, may create subjective artificial barriers in the child's mind and stand as a serious limitation on his hopes, aspirations and dreams. These barriers are created on the background of deep feelings of a lack of self-confidence, self-worth and self-efficacy. These barriers have nothing to do with the true potential of the child. As the child gets older, these barriers become more set and established in his mind and character, and the potential for change decreases. As a result, many people walk around with a sense of incompetence and miss out on their enormous potential. Building trust, esteem and mutual respect is the first step in empowering children from this kind of background. Providing a genuine sense of trust in the child and his abilities and creating successful experiences can certainly strengthen the child's basic belief in himself and his abilities. Each success produces a positive experience that reinforces the child's sense of confidence and capability, thereby increasing his belief in his abilities. At some point in this process, there is an Archimedean point where the child's deep sense of lacking becomes power, hunger and a tremendous urge for more success. The likelihood that a child who has passed such an Archimedean point will realize his full potential is especially high.

Following my personal story and the encounter with Prof. Bergman, it was clear to me that my private act of Tikkun Olam must be in the field of education, and must be related to children. After 13 years in the United States, the idea began to take shape. I was ready to become available for my own act of Tikkun Olam. First, I had to study the current situation on the ground: Are there any non-profit organizations operating in this field? If so, who are the leading organizations? Who stands behind them? What is their model? What is unique about each of them? What are the main challenges that they are coping with? What influence do they achieve?

The deeper I went into studying the current situation, the more I discovered that there are hundreds and thousands of organizations that deal with education. Like most Israelis, I also knew very little about the blessed social action that's going on in Israel. I was very surprised by the intensity of the work and the great quantity of well-meaning people and organizations. In the meetings I had, I became acquainted with good, generous, charming people who are committed to the idea that is closest to their heart. Moreover, they work day and night promoting it. Most of them are modest people who work hard, far from the limelight, to make the place we live in a better and more just place. These people, without a doubt, are the human capital and driving force of active civil society. They push for and promote the well-being of so many citizens, and therefore constitute an important and central element in the national-social resilience. The national poet, Chaim Nachman Bialik, wrote about these people in his poem, "Yehi Helki Imachem":[14] *"Your spirit is hidden inside of you like a pearl on the sea floor, and your capabilities, like the berries in the forest, hiding in the shadows of the shade."*

In order to better understand the connection between the establishment and the non-profit organizations and to hear the main problems facing the leading non-profit organizations in Israel, I went to a Knesset Education Committee discussion regarding educational organizations. I left the discussion with a few insights and a long list of the main organizations in Israel that deal with education. When I mapped out their geographic location, I was surprised to discover that the vast majority of the educational organizations operate in neighborhoods and communities in the centers of large cities or in development towns, which especially stood out in view of the lack of organizations operating in small and remote communities. Surrounding the development towns are many regional councils, which have included in them a great number of small and remote moshavs (small villages), but in reality, none of the non-profit organizations ever reach them. For example, in the cities of Netivot and Ofakim, where 28,700 and 24,600 residents live respectively, many non-profit organizations operate. In contrast, many small moshavs are scattered between and around these cities in a few regional councils, such as Sdot

Negev and Merhavim. Altogether, some 20,000 residents live in 32 small and remote communities; 16 moshavs in each regional council.[15] These small communities are given almost no attention by the educational non-profit organizations. Their remote geographic location and the limited number of children in each age group require a complicated logistics system and particularly expensive operating costs. This reality caused a lack of economic feasibility for non-profit organizations and associations to engage in educational activities in these locations. Non-profit organizations preferred to operate in disadvantaged neighborhoods in large cities and in development towns, where the number of children who can participate in activities is particularly large — which reduced the cost of the activity per child and gave economic justification for the activity. For example, in a small and remote moshav that has 10 to 15 children in a particular age group, the costs of operating an extracellular computer activity are much higher than the costs of operating the same activity for the same age group of about 40 children in a large city or development town. In addition, recruiting and transporting instructors in cities or development towns is easier and cheaper than in small and remote communities. Therefore, the exceptionally high operating costs caused almost all non-profit organizations to operate in more economically viable places, therefore avoiding the small and remote communities.

Each geographical unit in Israel — city, local council or regional council — is ranked by the Central Bureau of Statistics according to the socio-economic level of the population in that geographical unit. The socio-economic index is an important tool used by various government ministries and other central bodies in determining a policy of allocating differential resources to the local authorities. The geographic units in Israel are divided into ten clusters. In cluster 1, all of the geographic units are ranked with the weakest population, and in cluster 10, all of the geographic units are ranked with the strongest population. The socio-economic level expresses the integration of basic characteristics of the population in the same geographical unit. The term "socio-economic level" is perceived intuitively in its extreme situations: the poor at one end and the rich at the other end. For example, in 2013, only two municipalities were ranked in the socio-economic cluster 10: Savion and Kfar Shmariyahu. The financial means of the population is central but is not the only aspect of determining its socio-economic cluster. The other aspects are:

- The financial sources (from work, allowances, and other sources) of the residents.
- Housing - density, quality and other components in this area.
- Apartment equipment - such as air conditioner, personal computer and the like.
- The level of motorization (vehicles) - both numerical and qualitative.
- Education level.
- Characteristics of employment and unemployment.
- Socio-economic distress of various kinds.[16]

Communities of socio-economic cluster 5 and below are considered economically weak communities. The socio-economic level presents a good picture of the social problems and priorities in Israel. For example, an examination of the list of communities that are at the lowest socio-economic level, Level 1, indicates that most of them are Arab and a few are ultra-Orthodox. In fact, 45 of the 50 communities ranked in the lowest places are Arab, and five are characterized by the ultra-Orthodox population. According to the Central Bureau of Statistics data for 2013, Jerusalem, a city with 900,000 residents, was classified in cluster 3. These results sharpen the existing link in Israel between socio-economic gaps and a religious and ethnic background,[17] and undoubtedly constitute a badge of social poverty for the State of Israel. This is the result of inequality in the allocation of national resources and the neglect of the successive Israeli governments. In addition, the growing gaps between the remote locations and the center of the country are reflected in the fact that most of the large cities in the Central District — Herzliya, Kfar Saba, Petah Tikva, Rishon Lezion, Rehovot and Ra'anana — are in high socio-economic clusters 7 and 8. The absence of authorities is notable in the Tel Aviv District — except Or Yehuda and Bnei Brak — from the lowest clusters, 1 to 5. Overall, about 63 percent of the authorities in the center belong to the middle to high socio-economic cluster, between 6 and 10.[18]

The Central Bureau of Statistics does not publish the socio-economic ranking of the regional councils by level of locality (moshav), since most of the localities in the councils are too small to enable reliable estimates: approximately 50 percent of the localities in the regional councils amount to less than 500 residents and approximately 93 percent of the localities amount to less than 1,000 residents. On the other hand, the Central Bureau of Statistics does publish dispersion indexes for regional councils on the basis of the locality index. According to the Central Bureau of Statistics, most of the regional councils in the Southern District are in a socio-economic cluster between 5 and 7. Most of the regional councils in the Haifa District and Northern District are ranked in the socio-economic cluster between 4 and 7, and three regional councils are ranked in a low socio-economic cluster: between 1 and 3. All of the regional councils in the Judea and Samaria District are ranked in the socio-economic cluster between 3 and 7.[19]

It is important to remember that sometimes the affiliation of the regional councils to a socio-economic cluster is misleading and does not accurately represent all of the localities that are incorporated in that regional council. The difference in the socio-economic level of localities grouped under one regional council is likely to attribute it to a high socio-economic cluster relative to some of the localities that are incorporated there. For example, the Bnei Shimon Regional Council in the Negev combines 13 settlements — eight kibbutzes, one community settlement (Giv'ot Bar) and four moshavs (Brosh, Tidhar, Ta'ashur and Nevatim). There is no doubt that the socio-economic level of the four moshavs is significantly lower than the cluster in which the kibbutzes are classified as in this regional council and below the socio-economic cluster 6 — which is the general ranking of that regional council. Thus, I discovered that the small population in the remote settlements causes neglect by the state authorities, as well as the lack of attention among most of the educational non-profit organizations due to the high logistical costs required. Therefore, the population of children and youth in these remote and small localities seemed to me to be the most appropriate target population for my act of Tikkun Olam. I knew that if we were to succeed in finding a solution for the logistical problems that prevented most of the organizations from operating in these communities, it would be unique. The "small" problem remaining was to find such a viable solution.

In early 2003, on one of my trips to visit my parents in Be'er Sheva, I listened to a radio interview with the president of Ben Gurion University at the time, Prof. Avishai Braverman. The interview was held in honor of "Digital Gap" week in Israel, in which the reasons for the digital gap between those who use information technology and those who do not and ways to bridge this gap are usually discussed. The concept of digital gap refers to gaps in the adoption of information technology between different countries, as well as within countries between different parts of the population.[20] The concern for social justice and resilience is one of the factors that led countries around the world to work to narrow the digital gap. It was found that the digital gap is not random and, in fact, joins other social gaps that are correlated, such as housing, education, employment and income — a phenomenon known as "multiple discrimination."[21] During the interview, the interviewer asked Prof. Braverman what Ben-Gurion University is doing to reduce the digital gaps. Prof. Braverman proudly explained that the university, under his leadership, "just recently invested approximately $3 million in opening a computer lab for the welfare of children and youth in the area."

Prof. Braverman's statement sharpens the special problem of the population of children and youth in small and remote communities. The question that came to mind for me at that time was: what are the chances that a child who lives in a small, remote and disadvantaged community 20-30 minutes away from Be'er Sheva, will be able to benefit from the lab that they invested in at Ben Gurion University? The idea that a large family, at a low socio-economic level, living in a small and distant village and troubled by the difficulties of earning a living, will hear about the laboratory, allocate the time and resources necessary to drive the child back and forth — is a naïve thought. In the best-case scenario, the computer lab will serve a small portion of the children in the disadvantaged neighborhoods in Be'er Sheva, but most likely it will serve the children in Be'er Sheva who come from a high socio-economic level since they are the ones who have the necessary parental awareness and resources. Thus, for weeks after Prof. Braverman's interview, I kept thinking about the idea of making a computer lab, such as the one at Ben-Gurion University, available to the target population I had marked for myself — the population of children and youth in small, remote and disadvantaged communities. My technological background and understanding that education, especially technological education, is the best and quickest equalizer for closing social and economic gaps, pushed me to seek the desired solution.

Due to the high costs and the lack of economic feasibility, building a technological laboratory in every small and remote locality is not even a theoretical possibility, so how can new technological laboratories for children and youth be made accessible in these communities? After some time, I thought that if the children in the periphery could not be brought to labs in the center of the country, then perhaps the laboratories could be brought to the children in the periphery. This thought led to the idea of building mobile laboratories that could reach every location. A mobile laboratory would reach one community, give a class to a group of 18 to 20 children, then proceed to another community and give a class to 18 to 20 children, and so on. Access to technological education in the child's close and familiar backyard, together with his neighborhood friends, will make it easier and more pleasant for him to participate. Additionally, the mobility of the laboratory will also create a large virtual community that will consist of a collection of small communities in the scattered localities. By careful calculation, one mobile laboratory can give three to four technology classes per day to groups of 18 to 20 participants. It can expose between 270 and 400 children from small and remote localities per week to technological enrichment. The more I thought about the idea, the more enthusiastic I became, and the enthusiastic reactions and support I received from my friends encouraged me to further develop it. At one point, I decided to visit several regional councils in the Negev to hear from the local residents about their problems with informal education and to get feedback on our new idea on the subject. The first good sign was the warm welcome I received, although I felt their distrust of people from the "center" being interested in them without any other interests. To my joy, this distrust dissipated pretty quickly. In meetings with the heads of the regional councils and the directors of the departments of education and welfare, I confirmed the assumption that there was a severe lack of special enrichment and exposure activities and in their communities. Also, the reactions to the idea of mobile technology labs were very positive. In the Merchavim regional council, I met the head of the education department at the time, Shlomo Sharafi — a serious, charming, warm and kind person, and there was immediate chemistry between us. In the past, he was a principal of an elementary school in Be'er Sheva, and he knew the principal of the elementary school where I had studied. He got excited when I told him about myself and my motivation to take action for children from a background like mine and was enthusiastic about the idea of mobile labs. He joined in the effort on the spot and promised to do everything in his power to help us promote the idea in his regional council. Shlomo introduced me to the head of the council, and he, too, gave his blessing and enthusiastic support. Therefore, I decided that the ideal place for a "pilot" for the mobile laboratory would be the Merchavim Regional Council.

My friends and I decided to establish a non-profit organization for this purpose, and for that, we had to first give it a name. I thought the name should symbolize the essence of its activity. The Bible was the first source I turned to. When I came to a verse in the book of Ezekiel (1:20): "Wherever there was the will to go, they would go; there was the will to go, and the Ofanim (wheels) would lift themselves correspondingly to them, for the will of the living being was in the Ofanim (wheels)." I felt that it contained the main idea of the organization — it brought a new spirit, which is expressed in the last word of the verse — "Ofanim." This word has three different definitions, and all three of them describe the essence of the organization's activity:

1. "Ofanim" – wheels, which symbolizes the mobile laboratory.
2. "Ofanim" – forms, methods, ways, which symbolize the variety of technological enrichment activities that the organization will deliver.
3. "Ofanim" – in the Jewish tradition, this is one of the nicknames for angels, messengers of God. As, in a certain way, Prof. Bergman was an angel and a messenger for me, so too the counselors in the organization can be like angels for some of the children in these communities.

Thus, in December 2003, we, a group of good friends, submitted a request to open a non-profit organization called Ofanim — for the advancement of children and youth in Israel. The organization had set an objective of empowering children and adolescents from the distant periphery communities around Israel. The counselors — quality students who are full of motivation and a deep sense of a social mission — would give enrichment classes and expose the children and adolescents to science, technology and math using the mobile laboratories. The enlistment of my close friends for the opening of the organization was certain. Moreover, without their encouragement, urging and support, it's very doubtful whether Ofanim would have been established. Many of these friends became "crazy" about the idea, and to this day, they are the supporting pillar of the organization. The commitment, belonging and meaningfulness that each person in the group feels has made us a group that creates a model for working together and reinforcing the advancement of the goals of the organization. In addition, the joint activity brought us closer together, strengthened our friendship, added additional purpose and meaning and gave us the feeling that we are partners in something greater than ourselves.

In order to increase the chances of the success of the main idea of the organization, there is a need for people who deeply believe in the idea, adopt it, push and help promote it. The personal experience of each of the entrepreneurs, which led them to establish an organization or to be involved in it, also contributes to reliability and makes it very easy to enlist commitment to the idea. In addition, the ability to coherently, explicitly and clearly express the mission and the vision of the organization is very important. Forming a vision is the main lever for the management to cope with the complexity and uncertainty that characterizes the organizational environment in the present and in the future.

The vision is an organizing metaphor; it defines the

direction in which the organization strives to go, emphasizing the values, which serve as a guiding light. Beyond the vision are values that are the conscience of the organization. The mission defines the official reason for the existence of the organization and the main actions that the organization will carry out in order to ensure its existence over time. On the other hand, the vision is supposed to define the organization's modus operandi. The vision differs from the mission in that it defines the value system that guides the shared identity and purpose. The vision leads to the formation of commitment and purpose, and the mission leads to performing tasks and activities. Nevertheless, despite the complexity, it is necessary to define several structured stages of the process of creating the vision and implementing it in the organization's daily activities.[23] Clear and simple definitions of the vision and the mission help us focus on the problem we are trying to solve, which is to convey the message and enlist more "crazy" people for the idea. Careful and precise preparation in the early stages of the organization may remove many obstacles later down the road. The strong will and desire to begin to immediately take practical steps, without a clear formulation of the idea and without a thorough and professional examination of the field, can lead to many difficulties and even endanger the implementation of the idea. Therefore, in this case, it is very important not to let reason be the slave of desire. One must be patient and professional in the initial stages in order to study the problem, check its need in the field and clearly and accurately define it. It is essential to study the problem in detail. Knowledge, understanding and orientation of the problem convey the credibility and professionalism that are so necessary for recruiting supporters of the idea. In addition, becoming familiar with all the leading organizations working in the same field and a good understanding of the uniqueness of each organization's model and the challenges it faces, are also most vital; they help sharpen the message and uniqueness of the idea with other players and help recruit partners and supporters of the idea.

It is important to approach the problem from a position of humility. Real change is made in small steps and over time. For example, if the idea of an organization is to close social gaps in education, it should be limited to a specific geographic location or social group. Leaving the definition open, as if the organization has come to close all educational gaps in society as a whole, is too ambitious, not to say megalomaniacal. Of course, the aspiration behind every act of Tikkun Olam is for constant improvement. Yet, every change, as big as it may be, must start with small steps. After defining the problem and examining the true need in the field, it is necessary to connect and bind the target audience and the environment that we would like to work in to the target. Many of the social initiatives fail right from the start because those behind them have not been able to be attentive and sensitive to the real needs of the target audience. Only through full and genuine partnership with the target community can the desired improvement be achieved. This is especially true in educational organizations; the parents, teachers, school principals and local authority leaders know the subtleties, needs and demands of the community, and they know them better than anyone else. The idea that it is possible to come with a plan of action that is detached from the field and to implement it in the field without the deep involvement and partnership of the local community — is doomed to failure. This is why the Ofanim learning programs created joint groups composed of professionals from the organization, teachers, principals and parents from the communities in which we would like to operate. This is the reason that the learning programs in Ofanim were created by cooperative groups comprised of professionals in the organization, teachers, directors and parents from our target communities. This approach created trust, partnership and a positive atmosphere, and taught and gave us far beyond what we had come to give them. Over the years, Ofanim has enriched the lives of thousands of children from the remote locations, has exposed them to science, technology and math and has created many positive key experiences for them. The true linking-up and partnering of the business people from Israel and the United States for the funding and support of this activity are no less than the embodiment of the Zionist dream. For my friends and me, it is impossible for us to turn a blind eye to the enormous social gaps and continue as if we live in a vacuum. Still, we are not naïve. We understand that when it comes to social action, we apparently won't be able to change the whole world, but if we are successful in changing the world of even just one child — that is an ample return for our efforts. As our sages said, "Anyone who saves a life is as if he saved an entire world."[22]

# CHAPTER FOUR:

# BUILDING A BOARD
# OF DIRECTORS

*Leadership is the ability to define a vision and to energize others to implement it.*

- Jack Welch

# 1.

## HOW TO CHOOSE A BOARD OF DIRECTORS

Numerous studies that have examined the relationship between large corporations in the United States and the close ties between members of their boards of directors have led to the conclusion that these large corporations are intertwined and can be treated as a corporate community. The shareholders — wealthy families, bankers, accountants and lawyers — have contributed to the cohesion of this corporate community. Many of the large corporations established social and non-profit organizations with a goal of influencing their desired policy. Further studies have shown that there is a congruence between memberships in the boards of directors of corporations and memberships in the boards of directors of social organizations affiliated with these corporations. The organizations that comprise the corporate community and the network of its affiliated non-profit organizations provide the institutional infrastructure for the senior leadership group, which preserves the overlapping interests of members of the corporate community. Members of this closed group serve as members of the boards of directors or as trustees of corporations or non-profit organizations under the control of the corporate community by holding shares, financial support or serving in key positions in the board of directors.[1]

In this sense, the selection of members of the board of the affiliated NGOs of these corporations is based on shared interests and the preservation of cohesion and the similarity of the corporate community.

In light of the sparse research material on what is being done in Israel in this field, it is difficult to determine whether the situation in Israel is similar to that in the United States. It is reasonable to assume that as the field of philanthropy in Israel develops and matures, similar phenomena will emerge here as well. Already today, we are witnessing the emergence of self-interested "philanthropic" behavior in some of Israel's largest corporations. For example, it has become known that the "welfare" departments in some of the leading public corporations in the market collect "donations" (fees) from their employees and donate them to public institutions, such as hospitals. In return for the "donations," the employees of the "donor" corporations receive special — "welfare" — service in these public institutions, such as shortening their wait in lines, etc. These phenomena are fundamentally unacceptable. They pollute the public atmosphere and stain the name of philanthropy in Israel.

There are also people who want to serve on boards of directors of certain institutions because their intra-class status depends in part on the prestige of the board of directors in which they sit. The interest of these people is to perpetuate the board of directors as an exclusive elitist enclave, in order to nurture and preserve their status.[2] Our purpose in this chapter is to review the establishment of a board of directors for non-profit organizations that are defined as "philanthropy and volunteerism," especially in young organizations that were established in the framework of social involvement by people who want to socially influence from a pure and genuine motive, and not as part of a "corporate community" or an elite class group.

Like with start-up companies, many social organizations also fail and are shut down within a short period of time, not because of the main idea or the concept behind them, but because of mistakes made at the beginning — mainly mistakes stemming from lack of experience. Despite the strong desire and urge to act fast, there are steps in building a non-profit organization that should be carefully planned and invested in with great thought in order to increase the chances of success. These important steps constitute the infrastructure of the organization, and their meticulous planning may prevent anguish, wasting of resources and energy that are so important to the organization at the outset.

Management of the organization is done by the organization's various institutions. Each non-profit organization must set up at least three institutions: the general assembly, board of directors and audit committee. In organizations whose financial turnover is more than one million shekels — the exact amount is updated each year — there is another obligation, which is to appoint an accountant, in order to audit the organization's financial report. According to Chapter 4, Section 19a of the Amutot Law, "Every non-profit organization shall have a general assembly, an audit committee and may have additional institutions in accordance with the statute of the organization."[3] Among the organization's various institutions, the board of directors is the most important body. The board's official role is to manage the affairs of the organization, and it has all authority not mentioned in the Amutot Law or in the statute of the general assembly or in any other institution of the organization. The organization's general assembly selects the members of the board of directors unless otherwise determined by the statute of the organization. It is important to remember — choosing the right and appropriate members of the board of directors is one of the most important things for the success of the organization. The strong desire to progress in building the organization and to determine members of the administration in a haste and without deep thought may lead to a future compromise in the selection of appropriate members and cause obstacles and difficulties along the way. The board of directors has formal roles defined in the law — for example, Section 25 of the Amutot Law states that the board will manage the affairs of the organization and that it shall have any authority that is not specified in the Law or in the by-laws of any other institution of the organization. In practice, the roles of the board of directors are far beyond the management of the organization, first and foremost, the formulation and articulation of the organization's values, spirit and organizational culture.

In recent years, there has been a welcome phenomenon of senior executives and professionals from the business world transitioning to the boards of non-profit organizations. These people bring with them to the world of philanthropy experience, knowledge and advanced management methods, as well as important connections that can promote partnerships, involvement and higher support of non-profit organizations. This transition has the potential to improve management practices and increase the effectiveness of non-profit organizations. At the same time, it is important to remember that there are significant differences between the business world and the social world. As such, this transition also involves some difficulties stemming from the lack of understanding and recognition of the third sector and its uniqueness. This sometimes includes a lack of understanding of the organizational and legal structure of non-profit organizations, and a lack of familiarity with the changing rules of regulation and the complex relations between civil society, the government and the business world.[4]

Since social action is based in the first place on the values of social solidarity and mutual responsibility, moral and ethical conduct in non-profit organizations is a necessary condition. The organization must see paramount importance of ethics as an integral part of its management process. The success of ethical leadership is measured by its ability to cope with the challenge of optimal integration of the functional aspects and achievement of the organization's goals and the ethical aspects. It is very important that the goals and objectives for which the organization was established will be achieved, but it is equally important that members of the board of directors make sure that the path leading to achieving the goals is ethical. The moral obligation of each member of the board of directors must be fulfilled in all areas of his activity. The Amutot Law also states that every member of the board of directors has a fiduciary duty, which is to act solely for the benefit of the organization, and therefore he must carry out activities that serve the interests of the organization only and not his personal interests or those of his associates. A member of the board of directors must take into consideration the best interest of the organization and avoid any conflict of interest between his other areas of activity and the affairs of the organization. If such a conflict arises, he must fulfill the obligation of proper disclosure and report the conflict with full transparency.[5] The matter of the deep commitment of members of the board of directors is basic and of the utmost importance.

One of the most important roles of the board of directors is the responsibility and commitment to ensure that there is responsible, considerate and transparent management of the organization's resources. Since non-profit organizations operate from financial donations, that is, "with other people's money," the obligation of ethical, moral and transparent management is enormous. Improper, unwise and reckless use of the organization's resources is virtually the same as embezzlement, both in the role of the members of the board of directors and in the trust of the donors. Non-profit organizations that are not meticulously strict in their financial matters are abusing their positions and lose the moral basis for which they operate. The personal example set by the chairman or the CEO determines the organization's conduct in general and its financial conduct in particular. The genetic code of the organization begins with the personal example set by the chairman or the CEO. Excessive spending and inflated expenses by the chairman or CEO omits any moral ability to make claims to the members of the board of directors, or to any other position in the organization, about wastefulness or carelessness. Large salaries for position holders, transactions with interested parties, high compensation payments for participation in meetings, unreasonable reimbursement of expenses without checking and without auditing in some of the organizations — are among the main reasons for the bad reputation that has emerged in Israel. As far as the legislature is concerned, the organization is "fine" as long as it fulfills the basic rules of proper administration.[6] The irresponsible financial management of boards of directors in some of the organizations is also reflected in the strange demands of state institutions, which are based on total lack of trust in non-profit organizations. For example, as part of the audit process that the Ofanim organization underwent by the Registrar of Non-profit Organizations, the organization was asked to present a list of all the salary transfers made in recent years from the organization's bank account to employees. When the CEO of the organization asked the representative of the Registrar of Non-profit Organizations why he needed it, he responded, "We often find duplicate transfers to the same employees under slightly different names, or to fictitious employees." Inspection of the institutions is necessary and desirable, but no external inspection, enactment of additional laws or toughening the existing laws will change the situation and certainly will not correct the negative impression if the organization does not have a basic, clear, prudent and transparent code of conduct.

For these and other reasons, the general assembly of the

organization must select an audit committee or an auditing entity. An auditing entity may be an accountant or another entity approved for this purpose by the Registrar of Non-profit Organizations. This is one of the most important requirements for proper management. At least two members must serve on the audit committee, in accordance with rules of proper management. An auditing entity may be one person — an accountant or another entity that was approved by the Registrar of Non-profit Organizations. Most of the young non-profit organizations appoint an audit committee from among the members of the organization in order to save on accounting expenses. Some non-profit organizations see the auditing committee as a constraint of the legislation. In some of the various NGO boards that I've sat on, I often felt that the members of the board of directors felt uncomfortable asking questions about financial matters.

This problem is even more difficult in organizations in which there is not total transparency and is headed by a dominant chairman or CEO. More than once, I heard members of the committee claim that they did not feel comfortable challenging the chairman or the CEO out of the appreciation they felt for him. I don't understand this kind of appreciation that is built on idleness and misappropriation of the role. The opposite is correct: the obligation of the members of the board of directors must first and foremost be to the organization. With all the feelings of friendship and appreciation towards the chairman or the CEO, such irresponsible behavior is a betrayal of the trust of the organization, the donors and the target audience of the organization and to a large extent, it also harms the chairman or the CEO himself. A board of directors whose members or members of the audit committee feel too "uncomfortable" to ask about, check and examine all expenses and financial matters in the organization — is a not an efficient board of directors. Mature and professional chairmen and CEOs will prefer independent members of the board of directors that can challenge, question, examine and consult while at the table, over a group that just simply agrees with everything they say.

# 2.

## THE VITAL CHARACTERISTICS OF A NON-PROFIT ORGANIZATION'S BOARD OF DIRECTORS

The initial board of directors of the organization is comprised of the organization's founders. After that, the general assembly selects the board of directors, unless there is another instruction determined in the bylaws regarding this matter. The composition of the board of directors has paramount importance in determining the spirit and values of the organization and in forging its organizational culture. In other words, the composition of the initial board of directors constitutes the infrastructure and determines and establishes the genetic code of the organization. The members of the board of directors are like a mirror and serve as a personal example for the organization's professional staff. Members of the board who are unable to demonstrate ethical behavior in practice will not be able to implement it in the professional staff of the organization and demand that others behave in an ethical manner. Only a board of directors who identifies with the organization's idea and is fully committed to it will be able to implement the values and bring about the desired change that the organization is striving toward. Mahatma Gandhi put it well when he said, "Be the change that you want to see in the world."

Hence, it is of utmost importance to select the right and most appropriate people for the idea of the organization. This task is not at all easy, but it is critical for the success of the organization and for harnessing the environment — donors, supporters, volunteers, employees, etc. — to the underlying ethos and idea of the organization. The law itself requires that at least two members of the organization serve on the board so that the board can be built with patience and gradually. In addition to the person who constitutes the "extra soul" of the organization in the initial stages, who can be called "the first rib bone," the board of directors constitutes the second and most important rib bone for the success of the organization. The quality of the board of directors reflects the organization to the outside — donors, institutions, organizations and partners, and internally — the target audience and employees of the organization.

Nevertheless, it is important to ask — what makes a board of directors a good board of directors? It is common to think that the traits that characterize an active and alert board of directors are adherence to rules of proper management, the regular participation of its professional members in meetings, and activity according to orderly decision-making processes. Also, the composition of the board's committee must be balanced. However, contrary to this assumption, close observation of organizations and companies shows that adopting rules, processes and procedures for proper management is not necessarily a guarantee for success. This can be seen through the huge failures of giant companies such as Tyco Adelphia, Enron and WorldCom, where great attention has been paid to the boards of directors, yet they have still failed. So, the question arises — why did these companies fail? Is it a lack of professionalism among the members of the board? Did the boards of directors fall asleep while on guard duty? Did they cooperate with the corrupt administrations?

It was widely believed that these enormous business disasters could occur only in the face of negligent and even criminal behavior by members of the boards of directors, but a close examination of these boards revealed that in most cases it was not a lack of professionalism or corruption. In fact, these boards of directors acted in accordance with most of the accepted standards: the members of the board participated in meetings on a regular basis, and they invested their money in the companies they managed, so they had a clear personal interest in their success. In addition, there were audit committees, compensation committees and an ethical code of conduct. Although some of these companies did have a problem with the independence of some of its board members since they held a large number of internal board members as opposed to the number of external (independent) board members. Nevertheless, that was not true for all of the companies that failed. Moreover, in this respect, the composition of the board of directors was similar in companies that failed, compared to the composition in successful companies. Meaning, if the boards of directors of the companies had been examined with the standard tests used to determine whether they would succeed, they would have successfully met them.[7]

If so, how can a board of directors really be assessed? What are the qualities of a successful board of directors versus the qualities of a failed board of directors? Apparently, there is no simple and precise formula for this. The professional literature points to three main reasons for functional problems in a board of directors: the first is internal rivalries, dominance of some of the board members, one-way communication and lack of chemistry among members. The second is the lack of involvement of board members, which may stem from a lack of understanding of the organization's objective or lack of identification with it. The third reason is that not all committee members know and understand what their role is, out of confusion or lack of knowledge. Confusion or lack of understanding of the role, along with the dissatisfaction of board members, leads to a serious problem of feeling futile, of being uninvolved and of losing a sense of identification with the purpose for which they are sitting on the board of directors. The loss of a sense of identification with the objective of the organization is more severe than functional problems in the board of directors. Board members can know what to do and do it in a reasonable way, but in the end, if they feel frustrated by the futility of what they do, it will, of course, affect their functioning. In such cases, the definition of the role of the board members should be improved to include more attractive and significant tasks.

Section 25 of the Amutot Law grants the board of directors the authority to manage the organization. The powers of the board of directors and its roles are detailed in the

Registrar of Non-profit Organization's booklet "Guidelines for the Conduct of Non-Profit Organizations." This booklet includes a list of 15 sections that present the powers of the organization's board and its roles.[8] The definition of the role of the board of directors can be summed up in five main tasks that are imposed upon members of the board of directors:

1. To determine the organization's mission and overall strategy, and to change them as needed.
2. To examine the organization's performance and to demand accountability from the professional management.
3. To select the CEO, evaluate him, support him, and if necessary, replace him.
4. To develop and preserve the organization's resources.
5. To serve as a bridge between the organization and the community. To promote, build and expand community support in the organization.[9]

Section 27 of the Amutot Law states that members of the board have the responsibility "to act in the best interests of the organization within the framework of its goals and in accordance with the decisions of the general assembly."[10] It is important to remember that most of the formal work of the board of directors is episodic. Fortunately, not every meeting has strategic matters to discuss, such as selecting a new CEO or defining a vision. This "fiduciary" work of the board of directors is boring, but it is one of the most important tasks of the board of directors of an organization. A considerable part of the work of the board of directors is to control and supervise the professional management, in order to identify problems or deviations from the norms. The purpose of this role is to prevent theft, waste or misuse of the organization's resources and to ensure its maximum utilization, as well as to protect against unintended deviation from the organization's vision or an unauthorized shift from its goals. The board of directors must anchor in writing the arrangements and decisions related to the significant activity of the organization. According to the position of the Registrar of Non-profit Organizations, the roles of the board of directors include their responsibility to establish written procedures that regulate the organization's significant routine activities.[11] This work is no less important than working on strategic things, but sometimes it is boring and unsatisfying.

As stated, denial of this reality can lead to the loss of the sense of purpose and meaning among some board members. Therefore, it is very important to internalize the nature of the role of the board of directors. Full transparency, clear rules and processes are prerequisites for creating a positive reputation, which is the most important non-tangible asset of the organization. A positive reputation enhances the organization's ability to reach out to new audiences, hire good employees and attract donors. On the other hand, a negative reputation can be fatal. The adoption of procedures, rules and decision-making processes is a necessary but unsatisfying condition for the success of an organization.[12]

Above all, a good board of directors must lead. Leadership, according to the ninth president of the State of Israel, Shimon Peres, is not "to be high up," rather it is "to be ahead, to be in front." In 2015, in a meeting of the board of directors of Friends of Ofanim from the United States with Shimon Peres, he claimed that in his symbolic role as president he succeeded to influence more significantly and mobilize many more people than during his high, executive and authoritative position as prime minister. Leadership means, therefore, not the use of force or executive authority. Leadership in a non-profit organization must be based on moral authority. Such leadership leads to an organizational culture that allows and respects free critical discourse, tolerance, originality, credibility and non-coercion. The board of directors is meant to be the gatekeeper of the organization's ethos and values. It is supposed to shape the agenda, not impose priorities; to draw attention and not dictate results; to identify important opportunities and challenges, not demand specific solutions.[13]

Another necessary condition for a board of directors is its social fabric, one in which among its members there is mutual respect, appreciation and complete trust. This does not mean restraint or unanimity among the members of the board of directors but rather a firm and strong relationship that can contain challenging questions and opposing opinions. These conditions are necessary and may also be sufficient in business organizations and corporations. Board members of non-profit organizations, at least those who operate in the field defined as "Volunteering and Philanthropy," must feel a deep and genuine sense of belonging and commitment to the idea. They must fully identify with the organization's goals and create a social atmosphere that is pure, free of interest, open and positive. In such an atmosphere, board members can feel comfortable challenging each other out of practical considerations and can act with a deep and genuine commitment to advancing the organization's objectives.

The board of directors of a non-profit organization must also have something else, something I call the "pure space" — a place where people feel that they are part of something innocent, superior and bigger than them. A space that allows them to place themselves behind the objective and its service. The pure space is a place that connects and brings people to the purest and most genuine point within them, the point where they sense that they are partners in an innocent dream of a morally just and better world. It is hard to overstate the value of the pure atmosphere and the shared sense of the purpose and commitment of a group of people to a lofty idea and objective. Board members who meet in the pure space will be sensitive to any deviations from the established norm and will denounce any attempt to deviate from the code of conduct established as standard in the organization. For this purpose, on the one hand, the composition of the board of directors of a non-profit organization must be uniform in its morality, values and total commitment to the organization's idea. On the other hand, this composition must be varied in its areas of expertise and contribution to the advancement of the organization's objectives. In the selection of the initial members of the board of directors who share in the idea of the organization, it is very important to choose those with whom it is possible to create that pure space for the organization. A group of people that is connected based on the pure space has power that radiates at a great distance and has extraordinarily strong influence.

It is also important to remember that the law does not limit the number of members sitting on the board of directors. There are different opinions regarding the desired size of the board of directors in organizations. The prevailing view is that a small board of directors is considered good, whereas a large board is considered bad.[14] A board of directors with a small number of members can conduct concise and serious discussions and create a close and familial atmosphere, but the burden of managing and promoting the organization falls on the shoulders of a small number of members. On the other hand, in a large board of directors, many more people bear the burden, but it is difficult to conduct serious and concise discussions. In large organizations, there is also the need to set up various committees — for auditing, budgeting, investments, development, etc. — and a larger number of members enables time allocation and reasonable participation in committees. On the other hand, a large board of directors requires a large number of participants in each meeting in order to meet the requirement for a minimum "legal quorum." Indeed, the size of the board of directors depends on the volume of activity of the organization, yet, in most boards of non-profit organizations, the number of active members of the board of directors is limited. Generally speaking, it is not about the size, but rather the quality of the board of directors.

The addition of new members in young organizations in

its initial stages must be based on common characteristics — trust, values and identification with the objective — which will ensure the cohesion of the board during a period that is critical for the organization. There are also different opinions regarding the age of members of the board of directors; highly experienced board members can greatly contribute to the organization in its formation. Such members can be mentors to the young members who bring new energies and fresh thought. The integration of young people into the board of directors is also very important as part of building the next generation of the organization.

It can be said that in every organization, the board of directors must include members from four groups: donors, door-openers, professionals and the driving force (or "the living spirit"). Members of the board from the donors group are people with means and with high social awareness who are touched by the idea of the organization and are willing to bind themselves to the advancement of the organization's objectives and even contribute their money. The recruitment of board members who themselves are donors is a particularly difficult challenge for organizations that are just getting started. People with means and social awareness are courted by various organizations and associations, so most of them are already committed to one or more organization. One of the most important roles of the board of directors is enlisting donations and donors to the organization. The presence of donor members on the board of directors is a very important anchor, adding to the organization's sense of financial security. Donor members of the board have access to additional people with means from among their acquaintances who constitute a stockpile of potential donors. As the organization progresses and develops, the aspiration is for the board of directors to include as many donor members as possible. Donor members are very committed to the idea of the organization and usually have understanding and experience in various areas of the organization's management.

Nevertheless, sometimes having donor board members with a high socioeconomic profile may be an obstacle to additional donors for the organization; some potential donors use excuses like, "They do not need me, they have enough." Many non-profit organizations in Israel are founded by people with means and social awareness, who are the main and sometimes sole financial anchor of the organization. Since the organization is totally dependent on the money of the wealthy person, the wealthy person is also the influential person, and it is he who determines or dictates the tone of the organization. Such organizations are fully identified with their founder, for better or for worse, and there is a fine and delicate line between the professional needs of the organization and the desire and opinion of the wealthy person. In cases where this line has become blurred, the challenge of the board of directors to faithfully represent the needs of the organization is enormous. It is definitely important that the board includes donor members, but it is equally important that the organization not depend solely or mainly on the money of these members.

Members of the board from the door-opener group are well-known individuals whose names being listed on the board of directors gives weight, adds prestige to the organization and can help open doors for the organization to other institutions, organizations and potential donors. Such people give immediate recognition to the organization and its objectives, which is very important for non-profit organizations during their first steps. The recruitment of such people, who have integrity and public prestige, is not simple, especially for young non-profit organizations. These people are very busy and a large number of business and non-profit organizations court them. The chances of bringing such people to a young organization are possible if there is a personal connection to them. The real challenge is to bring a first-class door opener because, after that, it is easier to recruit additional door openers.

The board members from the professional group are experts in their field who can help the organization in the various disciplines involved in running an organization: legal, financial, public relations, etc. In addition, these board members should include domain experts in the organization's field of activity. It is easier for young organizations to locate and recruit members from the professional group than people from the door-opener and driving force group. The reason for this is that there are many good and generous professionals from various fields who are willing to lend a hand and join in the effort of the organization. When providing a strong motive, a clear vision and mission — recruitment from this group is relatively easy. A good and quality selection of members to the board of directors from this group can facilitate the recruitment of members from the other groups. Therefore, one must insist on choosing the best possible people from this group.

Finally, members of the board of directors from the driving force group are people for whom the idea of the organization is burning in their bones, almost like the founder or the "extra soul" of the organization. The driving force people are a kind of turbo engine that pushes and promotes the organization. Such people are relatively rare, but they will recruit their families, friends and the people around them and will give their all to promote the idea of the organization. The driving force people will always be available for anything related to the organization, and their enthusiasm is contagious and helpful when it comes to overcoming difficult times. It's very difficult to find such people. They are usually discovered during the organization's activities. An organization that has one or two board members of this kind is particularly fortunate, and its chances of success are especially high.

The classification of members of the board of directors into these four groups is very fluid and not dichotomous. Some people can be classified in more than one group. There are members from the driving force group who are also very professional. There are members who are donors who are also of the driving force, and those who are door openers and also very professional.

# 3.

## GOOD PEOPLE ALONG THE WAY

On the board of directors of Friends of Ofanim in the United States, I had the privilege and honor of meeting a unique woman named Amy Lipton. Amy was a successful lawyer with a big heart and a special soul, who fell in love with the idea of Ofanim and was one of the first to join the Friends of Ofanim board in the United States. Amy accompanied me to almost all of the many meetings we held with potential supporters on my many visits to the United States on behalf of Ofanim. Amy had a rare and staggering combination of qualities that enchanted everyone who met her: professionalism, energy, commitment, modesty, shyness, gracefulness, vitality, sensitivity and caring. It was impossible to meet her and not fall in love with her. She had a total and contagious commitment to Ofanim. Amy became, as the prophet Ezekiel said, "the living spirit in the wheels,"[15] and she was therefore called by all of the American board members "Amazing Amy."

Amy opened her wallet, her home and her heart — also the hearts of many of her friends — to the children of Ofanim. She did this from a humane, pure and genuine place: out of her deep and sincere concern for the future of Israel and its children. She embodied and symbolized the true essence of Ofanim in her character and personality. She was an "Ofan"— an angel — for thousands of children, even though the children of Ofanim did not even know her. It is hard to imagine Ofanim without Amy and her tremendous contribution to advancing the organization's objectives. Her devotion and commitment to Ofanim knew no bounds. Unfortunately, in 2015, Amy fell ill with a serious illness, and she passed away a year later when she was only 60 years old. Through her endless generosity and acts of kindness, Amy acquired an eternal place in our hearts and in the hearts of tens of thousands of Ofanim children. As I learned from my acquaintance with Amy z"l, one of the great and special gifts of social action is the amazing people we meet along the way.

When I was living in Atlanta, Georgia, I met Mr. Bernie Marcus, the legendary founder and owner of one of the largest and most successful "Do It Yourself" stores in the world — The Home Depot. This is a company of 2,269 stores that finished 2014 with revenues of 83 billion dollars! I met Bernie through his son, Michael, who was part of my social circle in Atlanta. One day, Bernie invited me to a meeting in which he asked me to help him recruit the Israeli businessmen in Atlanta to join the Israel Democracy Institute (IDI), which he had co-founded and was a supporter of. As far as Bernie was concerned, the significance of the Israelis giving their support was not from financial considerations, rather it was in Israelis taking responsibility for their society. Through my involvement in the recruitment of Israeli support for the "Democracy Institute," I got to know one of the most unique and inspiring women that I have ever met — Ms. Angelica Berrie.

Angelica was born on the island of Cebu in the southern Philippines and was educated in Catholic convent schools. For 22 years, she lived under the dictatorship of Ferdinand Marcos and joined the peaceful revolution movement that overthrew him. Arm in arm with nuns, a Bible held firmly in her hand and a prayer on her lips, Angelica stood tall and determined in front of the dictator's tanks, until he was forced to withdraw. In those days, Angelica could never have imagined that she'd leave her homeland, her religion and her family and marry Russell Berrie, a Jewish man born in the Bronx who produced gifts, toys, teddy bears and trolls for a living. The move from the Philippines straight to the heart of the Jewish community in New Jersey was not easy. Also, the fact that she was "Russ' wife" was accompanied by tremendous responsibility in the eyes of the Jewish community in general and the philanthropic community in particular. The concept of philanthropy was not part of her vocabulary. The concept of giving had been instilled in her at church, yet the meaning of it had been limited to placing something small in the collection basket during Sunday Mass. Angelica gradually became integrated into the community, met people and promoted various social issues, which enabled her to express herself and exposed her to the world of philanthropy.

Being part of an active and generous Jewish community that welcomed her with open arms and provided some exemplary figures who were a source of inspiration to her, led her to consider the possibility of converting to Judaism after ten years of marriage to a committed Jew who never obliged her to do so. She meant to surprise Russ and tell him about it on his 70th birthday, but unfortunately, Russ died the year before and had not seen her abandon her plan — as she had told him years before — to retire to the convent if she was left a widow. Angelica decided to convert after Russ' death because she had come to understand that she had already left the Catholic world that had nurtured her in her youth and she felt that her soul was drawn toward Judaism. Also, she had already become a committed and connected member of the Jewish community. In fact, many in the community thought she converted long before she actually did, as they could not imagine such a commitment without conversion. Angelica went through the process of preparing for conversion at the Shalom Hartman Institute in Jerusalem, where she personally studied Judaism with leading philosophers and scholars, such as Rabbi Prof. David Hartman, Rabbi Donniel Hartmen, Micha Goodman and others, who made her fall in love with Judaism even more. Since her conversion, she has spent every summer in Israel studying at the Shalom Hartman Institute and on trips throughout Israel, and she continues to learn from Israeli philanthropists who share the same values and desire to change.

After Russ' death, Angelica became the deputy chairwoman and CEO of the multinational, public company Russ Berrie & Co. Inc., which employed more than 1,600 employees all over the world. In addition, she became the president of the Russell Berrie Foundation. Angelica and Russ' interfaith connection led to the establishment of the Center for Interreligious Understanding, which brings together spiritual leaders of all faiths. As part of this effort, groups of imams and priests visit Auschwitz, and rabbis of all denominations meet with the Pope in the Vatican. The center has already trained seven interfaith cohorts from 21 countries: Catholic nuns and priests and laypeople. The fellows study at the Shalom Hartman Institute in Jerusalem and meet spiritual leaders from different faiths to promote understanding, tolerance, acceptance of the other, and building bridges between the various religions — so that in future generations members of other religions can live in peace with each other.

The Russell Berrie Foundation, headed by Angelica, supports many diverse projects in Israel: from the founding of the Russ Berrie Nanotechnology Institute at the Technion, to supporting the establishment of the medical school in Safed and the implementation of the "Tarbut Israel" project in cooperation with the Ministry of Education, which promotes the study of Jewish heritage and identity in high schools. Through the Russell Berrie Foundation, she enters into partnerships in social initiatives led by committed and dynamic leaders on issues that she considers having the potential for transformational change. "What I learned from Judaism," she once said, "is that even one act can change the world, that within which each one of us there is the power to reshape the world."

In Angelica's quiet, modest, sensitive and inspiring way, she has changed and shaped the world of many people in Israel and throughout the world. In 2007, Angelica joined the Board of Directors of Friends of Ofanim and in 2014, she took on the role of Chairwoman of Friends of Ofanim in the United States. Her commitment and concern for the children of Ofanim and the strengthening of the periphery in Israel are enormous and absolute. Beyond the amazing work that Angelica is doing to promote and support the organization, she is a source of inspiration for members of the board of directors both in Israel and the United States. Through her social action and deep commitment to Israel and the Jewish people, Angelica symbolizes the modern version of Ruth the Moabite. Indeed, after her conversion, Angelica took on the Hebrew name "Ruth." The name of her mother-in-law, the mother of her husband Russell Berrie *z"l*, was Naomi.

In Israel, there is a faulty practice in which most of the heads of non-profit organizations fill their roles indefinitely. One of the reasons for the negative impression on non-profit organizations stems from the widespread feeling that some of them constitute a kind of permanent work arrangement. The law in Israel does not limit the maximum period that a chairman or CEO can hold office, and therefore, there are organizations in which the CEO or chairman serve in the position for long periods of time, making them very dominant and thereby undermining the important balance between the executive committee and the professional staff. In addition, there are many non-profit organizations in which the veteran and dominant CEO appoints the chairman and the board of directors. This situation is not healthy because it does not allow real balance and control of the organization's activity. A voluntary limitation on the period of tenure by the non-profit organizations will lead to improved activity, transparency and increased public trust in non-profit organizations. There is nothing healthier and more refreshing for an organization in general, and for a non-profit organization in particular, than restricting term limits for senior executives, including members of the board of directors, the CEO and the chairman. One of the common misconceptions in organizations is that there are key people in the organization that are simply "indispensable." In this context, the cliché that "the cemetery is full of irreplaceable people" is very accurate. New blood flow, new management methods, new styles and new energies are the oxygen of an organization and are necessary in a changing world like ours. The ability to move forward, to be free of habits and organizational fixation, is possible only by limiting the length of time that key people in an organization can serve in the same position.

The role of the founder is to be the "living spirit" in laying out the vision, to nurture and create the "pure space," to choose the initial members of the board of directors, to establish the genetic code and build the foundation of the organization. The founder of the organization is like an entrepreneur of a start-up company; he has the vision and the drive to make it happen. But in many cases, the entrepreneur is not the best person to manage the company after it has developed, ripened and matured. The true strength of an organization is measured when it continues to operate and develop, even when the founder is no longer the person holding the steering wheel. Moreover, sometimes organizations grow to new heights precisely when the founder is no longer the leader.

One of the difficulties faced by organizations in general, and non-profit organizations in particular, is the leadership continuity. For this purpose, limiting the term of office of the chairman, the board of director's members and the CEO, and the inclusion of young people on the board of directors and nurturing them as a reserve for the management of the organization, are vital and necessary. Founders must always remember the ultimate goal of the organization and be careful not to fall into the "Owner's Trap." Meaning, one must be aware of an absolute identity between the founder and the organization, an identity that prevents any possibility of new leadership growth.

In light of the tremendous importance of term limits for the board of director's members, including the position of chairman, I declared in the first board of director meetings of Ofanim my intention to serve for a limited period. Ten years, at most, seemed to me a reasonable period of time in the same role and the appropriate amount of time for new blood flow for the organization. Approximately three years before the end of my allotted time, we began to look for a candidate for chairman of Ofanim. The process of transferring the reins is delicate and exceedingly important for any organization. In order to create continuity and to make the transition as smooth as possible, the replacement chairman should be accompanied by a long overlapping process. The fact that I did not intend to leave the organization, rather just the position, enabled us to search for the most suitable person without the time pressure and to carry out an orderly overlapping process. Choosing the wrong person can create agitation and irreversible damage, especially for a not-so-big organization like Ofanim. Therefore, we looked for a candidate who shares the values of the organization, has good human relations, understanding and experience in the field and can connect to the "pure space" we created. The role of the chairman, in every organization, is a demanding role that requires enormous time, energy and resources, all for no pay. For this, it must be a suitable person who sees social involvement as a deep personal commitment. And, as expected, the task proved to be a particularly difficult task. Few candidates were able to afford the time and energy required for the job, without receiving any financial payment.

After a long search process and one unsuccessful attempt, we chose Mr. Oded Hadomi to serve as the chairman of the organization. The story of how Oded came to join Ofanim is a moving and inspiring story. As part of the operation of Ofanim, each mobile laboratory works in cooperation with an institution of higher education: The Robotics Laboratory works in cooperation with the Technion, the Astronomy Lab with Ben-Gurion University, the Lab for Young Physicians with the Medical School in Safed and so on. Some of the Ofanim science activities take place in institutions of higher education, in order to expose the children to these institutions, remove artificial barriers, strengthen their self-confidence, and instill in them the belief that they can learn in these institutions in the future. One of the first institutions to cooperate with Ofanim was the Shenkar College of Engineering and Design. During my first visit to Shenkar, I met with the CEO of the college at the time, Mr. Baruch Sagiv, in order to enlist the college in partnership with Ofanim. Baruch was very enthusiastic about the idea that children from the periphery would visit the college and participate in workshops in the college laboratories and in various engineering fields. He presented the matter to the directors of the various laboratories, who unanimously agreed to give the workshops on a fully volunteer basis.

I asked Baruch to appoint a contact from the college to coordinate the visit with the organization, and he offered a young student named Oded Hadomi, who was the chairman of the student union at Shenkar at the time. He noted that Oded had "a high social awareness" and, in his opinion, was the most suited for the task. But he added that Oded was in the final stages of completing his degree and had already started working in a high-tech company, so he was not sure he would be available. Baruch accompanied me to meet with the director of the cafeteria at the college to close the details for lunch for the children of Ofanim during their planned visit to the college. As we walked into the cafeteria, we happened to bump into Oded, a tall and skinny man, who had just arrived to close up some final matters at the college. "Here's the guy I told you about," Baruch cried out. And already then, in my first encounter with Oded, I was fascinated by this modest, quiet and composed young man.

His immediate devotion to the matter was from the recognition of the importance and significance of the visit for the children. Even though he was still in college, and at the start of his professional career in a demanding high-tech job, Oded agreed to take on the role and enlist some of his colleagues to the matter. Thus, for several weeks, I worked with him in the preparation of the children's visit to the college and was exposed a little bit to his captivating personality and amazing management abilities. During the time of the preparations for the visit, Ofanim was then at the height of the process of finding a CEO for the organization. After several months of an intensive search, the Search Committee selected two candidates who reached the final screening stage. After the children of Ofanim's moving and successful visit to Shenkar, I shared my impression and my enthusiasm for Oded with the board, from the professional way in which he had managed the visit, and I proposed that the search process be stopped and an examination of whether Oded was suited to be the CEO of the organization. Some of the committee members who participated in the Ofanim children's visit to the college also met Oded and expressed their enthusiastic support of the idea. Thus, the board instructed me to find out what Oded thought of the matter.

From my short acquaintance with Oded, I knew that he was the most suitable for the job, but I assumed it would not be easy to persuade a young man who had just finished his studies in engineering to change direction from the promising and rewarding technological field to the field of social action. A few weeks after the children of Ofanim's visit to the college, a special visit that became a tradition for many years, I met with Oded in my office. After thanking him for his substantial help in preparing the successful visit, I proposed that he be the CEO of the organization. Oded was very surprised by the proposal, and as I expected, he claimed that he had just started working in the high-tech industry and was not sure that moving to the social field at this stage would not be a serious blow to his professional career. The wage gaps between the field of high-tech and what a small and young non-profit organization could offer were not in my favor either. After he rejected all my attempts to rationally convince him, I turned to the emotional argument, which I believed might tip the scales.

"Oded," I said to him, "I do not know if your move to the social field will hurt your professional career, nor can I offer you a high salary like in high-tech career, but I can promise you two things that you will get from the move to the social field. Two essential things, no less important and even more important. And what are these two things? By engaging in social action, you will get an important perspective on life that few people get at such a young and formative age. This perspective will expand your awareness and give you balance, satisfaction and real meaning in your life. The second thing is that in social involvement you will meet good, interesting and special people, some of whom will be true friends for life. These are two important and essential gifts that, if you are smart enough to accept them, you will thank me for it in the future." After a long silence, he answered, "Before I consider the matter, I want to examine Ofanim's activity in the field." I sensed that I had touched a sensitive spot, which had created the first crack in the wall. After the visit in the field and endless questions about the organization, its goals, objectives, etc., we met again in my office to hear his answer. "You should know that I was very surprised by your request.

As you know, I served as an officer in the IDF and contributed two additional years beyond compulsory service. After meeting the children in the periphery, I feel I have again been called to duty. I see this as another important contribution, no less than my career military service to the country. I'll take on the position, I'll only commit to three years, and I hope I will not lose my professional future because of it." I sat across from him, thrilled and excited, and I said to myself, "Blessed are the people, that these are its sons."

Oded began his position as CEO of Ofanim in 2007 and finished, as he promised, exactly three years later. During this period, Ofanim grew and developed by any standard and became one of the leading non-profit organizations in the field of informal education in Israel. After three years as CEO, Oded returned to the high-tech field, and today he is the CEO of a start-up company in the field of medical devices. About a year after leaving Ofanim, he joined the board of directors. In 2015, he was called to duty again, this time as chairman of the organization. As a young chairman, Oded brought with him a new and refreshing style, and even enlisted additional young forces to the professional team and the board of directors, bringing new momentum to the organization. About a year after his appointment as chairman, Oded told me that when he complained to a close friend that between his various obligations — to the family, to the job as CEO of a start-up company and to the position of chairman of Ofanim — he could not find time for anything else, his friend suggested that he consider quitting Ofanim. "Ofanim," Oded replied, "is part of me, part of my identity,

part of what defines me. How can I break away from myself?"
I hugged this charming and exciting young man, who from
the moment he joined Ofanim, was like a younger brother to
me. A good, wonderful man along the way.

# CHAPTER FIVE:

# FUNDRAISING

*The value of a man should be seen in what he gives and not in what he is able to receive.*

- Albert Einstein

# 1.

## BACKGROUND AND PREPARATION

Fundraising is the most important mission in a non-profit organization, and every member of the organization must be aligned with it. In order to succeed in this task, one must work professionally and according to orderly processes. The organization's message must be clear, catchy, adapted and up to date with current support trends. The intense competition amongst many organizations for the limited resources is growing. Rachel, the late Amy Lipton's sister, gave this competition the spot-on name "Competition of Sorrows." In this difficult "Competition of Sorrows" over the resources, there is a huge advantage to non-profit organizations that are led by credible leaders who identify with their goals and promote an exciting idea with potential for serious influence. People donate to people, not to institutions, so the credibility and chemistry between the donor and the person asking for the donation is critical in achieving the donation. The potential donor must feel confident that the organization's leaders can, in fact, leverage his contribution to advancing the goals of the organization with which he identifies. The potential donor has various motivations for giving: a sense of belonging to the community, a sense of satisfaction and enjoyment from the act of giving, a family tradition of giving, a sense of responsibility of the donor to his surroundings, a connection to certain topics and his personal interest in them, etc.[1]

In order to know where to allocate his contribution, the potential donor, whether private or institutional, must decide which of the many goals before him is the most pressing or important to him. Contrary to traditional donors who have donated to general, important and lofty goals but without meticulous scrutiny of their donation and its results, the new donors — those who have made their fortunes in high-tech and other advanced industries — are rationally, prudently and carefully donating to specific goals and objectives. They aren't donating their money for undesignated general purposes. The new donors are goal oriented and seek to be involved in the social and civil programs and initiatives that they donate to. These donors, who were educated in private and business systems, adopt the business management pattern to manage their social donations — their investments. They not only give their money but expect a return on their investment in social terms and in the measure of impact that investment has on society and the target audience.[2] The involvement of these new donors carries a great promise of more transparent, orderly and efficient conduct.

As stated, the future of each organization depends, to a great extent, on the ability to fundraise. Many organizations in Israel start their way with a great call of the trumpet and cease their activity within two to three years with a weak response, which is a result of their inability to fundraise. This is the main reason that only about 15,000 of the more than 40,000 non-profit organizations — including public institutions — that are registered in Israel are active.[3,4] In addition, each year more than 1,500 new organizations are added to this competition for the limited resources.[5] The rapid increase in the number of non-profit organizations (NGOs) and the recognition of their importance in society, as well as the institutionalization processes that followed these processes — legislation, public policy, academic research and teaching, and the establishment of infrastructure organizations and umbrella organizations — were not accompanied by public discussion of their place and role in society. The uniqueness of NGOs in relation to other organizations in the business and public sectors is in the non-profit goals, in the prohibition of distribution of profits, in being assisted by volunteers and donations, and in their legal status. These led to their classification and cataloging as a separate sector: the third sector, or the social sector.[6]

As noted, although a large part of the Israeli public has a positive view of the activities of the non-profit organizations, there is still a wide negative sentiment towards the third sector. The lack of culture and education for giving, the widespread public suspicion of the giving of those have the ability to, and the difficulties in evaluating the effectiveness of non-profit organizations — still constitute major barriers to giving in Israel. These and other barriers were also reflected in the results of the 2015 "Global Giving Index" of Israel's non-profit organizations, in which Israel ranks 72nd out of 145 countries in volunteering, donating and assisting foreigners.[7] This place is far from being a worthy place for a people whose values and heritage are based on kindness and helping others. The experience of countries with established and developed philanthropic culture shows that in order to advance and develop the culture of giving, four challenges must be met:

1. Legal and economic restrictions and barriers on philanthropy and on the third sector.
2. Values and cultural perceptions that do not accept or understand the role of philanthropy and the third sector.
3. Limited involvement of citizens in philanthropy.
4. An undeveloped social infrastructure to support donors and potential donors.

We have already noted that the prevailing cultural perception in Israel sees the state as solely responsible for dealing with social problems. This is one of the reasons a large part of the public does not contribute to non-profit organizations.[8] The role and responsibility of philanthropy in Israeli society is still developing and is not as wide-spread as in the United States, for example. Unfortunately, this perception also affects how most of the rich perceive their social responsibility.[9]

Nevertheless, quite a few things have led to extensive philanthropic activity in recent years: the profound changes in welfare policy, hegemony in the neoliberal economy, the enormous social gaps, changing social needs that are not met by the government, the decline of the public education system, the rapid accumulation of new wealth and the growth of the third sector.[10] This activity is driven by, among other things, a feeling of solidarity and social commitment towards the weaker segments of society. This moral-ethical obligation motivates people and organizations to take action for the weak and the needy. This action, of course, includes donations of money, or monetary equivalent — "in goods" — along with volunteer activities.

A person who acts as a fund-raiser for an organization must feel an absolute identification with the goals of the organization for which he is acting, otherwise, he is betraying himself. The fund-raiser must determine, in the most honest way, whether he understands the meaning of fundraising, and whether he is truly prepared for the enormous responsibility of the meticulous and precise handling of other people's money. Because non-profit organizations operate through donations, that is, with the money of others, the commitment to straight, honest, ethical and transparent conduct is enormous. The giving of financial donations to non-profit organizations by donors, whether private or institutional, is a complete and unconditional expression of confidence in the organization and in each of its directors. Receiving a donation — any donation, from a private person or institution, and in any sum — must be regarded by members of the organization as an act of special value that is not self-evident. In other words, the fact that people open their hearts and pockets and part with it at their own free will is impressive and wondrous, like a miracle.

Improper, unwise and careless use of donor funds is virtually the same as embezzlement of the donor's trust. It also causes injustice and wrongdoing to tens of thousands of honest and wonderful people who work day and night doing holy work in various organizations. Newspaper headlines about corruption and unjustified huge salaries of a handful of NGO directors have caused damage, created a distorted picture and tarnished the name of the entire third sector. Also, the increasingly stringent legislation stems from the governing institutions' lack of trust in the third sector and the public atmosphere caused by the irresponsible behavior of some of the organizations and their directors.[11]

There is a lack of trust and cynicism among many in Israeli society, which has led to the common belief among the public that no action can come from a place that is genuine, clean and pure. There must be a hidden interest. Due to the negative impression of non-profit organizations, good people have asked me countless times, "How much do you earn in the non-profit organization?" There is a lack of trust in their faces when I answer, "Nothing, the board of directors does its work on a voluntary basis." I also grasped the extent that the public holds this negative view in a meeting that I attended two years ago at the Ministry of Education in Jerusalem, about a potential partnership between Ofanim and the Ministry of Education. Around the huge oval conference table sat various representatives of the Ministry of Education, headed by the General Director of the ministry. At the beginning of the meeting, I was asked to present myself, the other representative and the activities of the organization. After I did so, the General Director asked me, "What do you get out of all this?" After taking a deep breath, I replied, "Although I have been asked this question more than once before, I must say that I did not expect to hear it from the General Director of the Ministry of Education. As strange as it may sound to you, I am part of a large group of citizens who feel a deep commitment to trying to make our country a better place."

Those who are involved in social action in Israel know from reality how far this negative impression has gone, and what enormous damage it is causing to so many people, institutions and organizations. These damages and the negative impact on nonprofit organizations are a serious stumbling block in the path of philanthropy in Israel and are some of the main obstacles to raising funds, enlisting volunteers and others to join organizations. We must admit that some of the blame falls on our shoulders — the members of the boards of directors of the non-profit organizations. Over the years, I also met non-committed people who did not contribute much to the non-profit organizations but merely decorated their names with "member of the board of directors." Their participation in administrative meetings was casual and non-contributing, and in some cases even burdened the organization's expenses — with compensation for participation, travel, etc. In certain cases, budgets and expenses presented by the professional staff were approved almost automatically, without serious discussion and without examination and investigation by members of the board of directors. In some non-profit organizations, inappropriate and unreasonably large salaries were paid. As far as the legislator is concerned, the organization is "fine" as long as it fulfills the basic rules of proper administration, according to which "the organization is entitled to pay a salary that is more than reasonable, taking into account the employee's qualifications and that which is accepted in the labor market for similar functions," and "in regard to setting a wage ceiling for the salaries of senior managers in non-profit organizations, the reasonableness of wages is examined while taking into account the following factors: the annual turnover of the organization, independence, effectiveness of management and the quality of the position holder."[12]

It is clear that the salaries of senior officials in the professional staff of non-profit organizations is a sensitive matter and must be taken into consideration. The competition for quality human resources on the part of businesses that can afford to offer huge wages leaves non-profit organizations with very low chances. Human resources are the most important resource for any organization, social or business, and in order to attract talented and high-quality people, organizations must offer competitive but reasonable wage levels. Salary cannot be detached from the organization's budget and from the extent of the responsibility that accompanies the job. Social action is an area in which the ethical, moral and value-oriented statement is very important. Without this moral statement, the organization loses the foundation of its existence. Therefore, the entry of non-profit organizations into free wage competition like in the business world is misplaced and sends the wrong message. In addition, particularly high salary levels will inevitably put a question mark on the real motives for the social involvement of these senior managers. Non-profit organizations need to find the right balance in recruiting the highest quality and most talented people at reasonable salary levels that are consistent with the values they are trying to promote. There are many talented people with high social awareness, who are seeking to make a change and move from the business world to the social world. Many of them are aware and are willing to compromise on the salary level.

As part of the struggle against the distorted impression and the good reputation of the non-profit organizations, we — entities like Committed to Give, the JFN, Midot, Sheatufim, GuideStar and others — have to be more assertive about the demand for maximum transparency and be vocal against those who abuse their status. We must compose a code of transparency and rules of conduct regarding donors' money, as well as determine that the salaries of senior officials in non-profit organizations will be much more rigid than what the law requires. In addition, we must ask all NGOs to adopt these rules and publish the list of non-profit organizations that are committed to adopting this code of conduct. A voluntary and rigid code of conduct emerging from the third sector, which will serve as a basic measure of transparency, integrity and incorruptibility, is a moral and ethical statement that has the power to correct the widespread negative impression amongst the public. Such a clear statement can also help us root out the weeds, enlist other entrepreneurs to social action and bring the message and hope of philanthropy to greater parts in Israeli society. Full transparency and the use of the donor funds with fear and trepidation is a supreme moral and ethical duty, not only to generous donors but to the entire social sector.

# 2.

## MAIN SOURCES OF INCOME AND FINANCING

As we have already noted, the common perception among many people in Israel is that the state is solely responsible for all social affairs. In addition, life in Israel — which includes high taxes, reserve duty, etc. — reinforces this perception. However, due to the strong general economic situation of the State of Israel in recent years and the many successes in the high-tech industry, in particular, many Israelis have accumulated enormous capital. As a result, the number of potential donors in Israel has significantly increased. Positive signs of change can be found in the ever-increasing desire of wealthy individuals and families to learn more about strategic philanthropy and venture philanthropy. In addition, the developing "corporate social responsibility" and the role of a market economy aimed at social and community issues are also a great opportunity for new social initiatives and other resources.

Despite the development of Israeli philanthropy, a large number of companies and individuals are still not involved in philanthropy in Israel, relative to the rest of the world. In 2014, Israeli philanthropy accounted for 0.87 percent of the GDP, compared to 2 percent in the United States. Only 15 percent of Israel's citizens participate in volunteer activities, compared to 25 percent in the United States, 50 percent in England and Canada, and 30 percent in Australia, Holland and Germany. In addition, only nine percent of Israeli corporations contribute to the community as part of the "corporate social responsibility."[13]

The main sources of income of non-profit organizations are grants and subsidies from the state, as well as the sale of services and donations or transfers from the private sector. Every organization's aspiration is to obtain support from all major sources of income, but this requires much time and resources. Therefore, in the early stages, the members of the organization must decide on the source in which they invest their best efforts to raise funds, and in which they have the highest chances of achieving the fundraising targets that they have set for themselves. In order to succeed in the mission, the organization must study the various sources and the support trends — education, welfare, etc. — of various sources, and see how the organization's message can be adapted to these trends. There should be constant and continuous tracking of the support trends of the various sources. Advance knowledge of the support trends enables early preparation of the organization and improves its chances of benefiting from a change in these support trends.[14]

In 2014, the gross product of the NGO sector — the added value of this sector to the economy — was around 5.5 percent, which is 59.7 billion NIS, of the gross domestic product in Israel, and it employed approximately 450,000 employees — about 13.6 percent of the employees in the economy. The total income of NGOs in Israel amounted to

132.6 billion NIS, of which 49.7 percent was from government transfers, 32.8 percent from sales of services, 15 percent from donations from Israel and abroad and 2.5 percent from interest and property. In 2014, there was an increase of 3.8 percent of total revenues compared with 2013, in relation to a rise of 5.7 percent in 2013 compared to 2012.[15]

### TABLE 4

### NGO incomes according to source of financing

*in millions of NIS (2009-2014)*

| Year | Total income | Government transfers | Sales of services | Dona-tions | Interest and roperty |
|------|--------------|----------------------|-------------------|------------|----------------------|
| 2009 | 106,717 | 50,414 | 34,151 | 19,771 | 2,381 |
| 2010 | 113,216 | 53,418 | 36,217 | 21,048 | 2,533 |
| 2011 | 122,230 | 57,818 | 39,027 | 22,651 | 2,735 |
| 2012 | 120,977 | 59,758 | 39,844 | 18,311 | 3,064 |
| 2013 | 127,787 | 63,547 | 41,885 | 19,115 | 3,240 |
| 2014 | 132,556 | 65,793 | 43,522 | 19,888 | 3,353 |

*Source: The Central Bureau of Statistics*

As is reflected in the table, close to 50 percent of all non-profit organizations' income comes from transfers from various government ministries. The lion's share — about 60 percent of this income — is for non-profit institutions that are defined as public institutions: HMOs, institutions of higher education, etc. The total income of NGOs with the deduction of public institutions is about 40 percent of the total income of NGOs in Israel. For example, in 2011, the total income of NGOs excluding public institutions amounted to 46.26 billion NIS, about 38 percent of total income in that year.[16]

One of the most prominent advantages of a non-profit organization is its ability to receive recognition by the Income Tax Authority as a public institution for donations, under section 46a of the Income Tax Ordinance. Such recognition enables an organization that is a public institution and meets the rules set for obtaining a certificate entitling donors to the organization to a tax benefit for their donations. The taxable donation range is between 190 NIS and the lower of these two: 9,295,000 shekels or 30 percent of the taxable income for that year. The tax credit is 35 percent of the donation amount of an individual and 25 percent ("corporate tax") of the donation amount of companies. It is very difficult and almost impossible to raise funds for an organization without receiving income tax recognition from the Income Tax Authority.

For most companies and organizations, approval under 46a of the Income Tax Ordinance is a necessary condition for giving a donation. Many private and public donors see this recognition as a kind of kosher seal. Therefore, one of the first important tasks that an organization must do immediately upon its establishment is to initiate the process of recognition by the Income Tax Authority regarding donations. The procedure for receiving Section 46a approval is a long process — lasting more than two years — and it's expensive but absolutely necessary. Of all the non-profit organizations operating in Israel in 2011, less than a third

— only about 4,280 — are recognized by the Income Tax Authority as a public institution for donations under Section 46a of the Income Tax Ordinance, which grants their donors recognition for tax purposes.[17] Of all the approvals granted by the Tax Authority in Israel, 27.9 percent were given to organizations operating in the field of religion, 25.4 percent to organizations in the field of education and research, 18.2 percent to welfare, 10.2 percent to culture and leisure and 3.7 percent to health.[18]

In addition to the services that the government "purchases" from non-profit organizations — "outsourcing" — which constitute about 50 percent of the income of non-profit organizations in Israel, a relatively small number of non-profit organizations also receive government support for their activities. For years, this support was granted arbitrarily and not transparently. Until the beginning of the 1990s, the scope of support for each organization was determined in detail in the annual state budget law, without any clear and constant criteria or standard. A large part of this support was a sort of distribution of "biscuits" by politicians to the groups that they are connected to. This phenomenon was given the name "the unique funds" and received harsh public criticism. In light of the criticism, and the fact that these are state funds being given to private entities, in 1992, the Knesset enacted Section 3a of the Budget Foundations Law, in order to establish rules for distributing the support funds in a transparent and clear manner. Despite the amendment to the law, even today it is very difficult for an organization to receive government support under section 3a, unless it has connections with politicians who really like it.

In regard to transparency as well, the distribution process did not change much.[19] For example, in the budget discussions at the end of 2016, the Ministry of Finance decided to disclose the names of the politicians who are behind allocations under this section in order to cause them "to be ashamed," thus minimizing the distribution of the "unique" funds. But the boasting in the media of many of the politicians whose names were published as recipients of "unique" funds shows that the opposite effect was achieved — instead of being ashamed, it seems that a competition had begun between politicians who see the size of the achievement in as much as they managed to extort money from the treasury as "unique funds" in exchange for their support for approving the budget. Over the past decade, government support for a relatively small number of NGOs, which are not public institutions under section 3a of the Budget Foundations Law, has stood at an average of 2 billion NIS per year.[20] A large portion of government support under this section is done through two ministries: the Ministry of Education and the Ministry of Culture and Sport.

### TABLE 5

## Support of the Ministry of Education and Culture of NGOs under Section 3a of the Budget Foundations Law

*(according to the data of supporting ministries in 2006-2014)*

| Year | Ministry of Education-support of religious institutions | Ministry of Culture and Sport |
|------|------|------|
| 2006 | 699,347,000 | 420,069,184 |
| 2007 | 825,780,000 | 442,769,480 |
| 2008 | 849,439,000 | 483,075,391 |
| 2009 | 974,097,717 | 516,418,286 |
| 2010 | 1,030,999,477 | 503,364,332 |
| 2011 | 896,958,579 | 565,562,045 |
| 2012 | 1,033,980,052 | 671,284,767 |
| 2013 | 757,095,890 | 551,762,133 |
| 2014 | 576,094,095 | 568,328,313 |

*Source: Ministry of Education and Culture*

More than half of government support under section 3a goes to religious institutions. An examination of the list of institutions receiving government support under section 3a also found institutions that are not recognized by the Income Tax Authority as public institutions for donations. Although the government does not need tax recognition, this recognition adds a level of control for more proper conduct, which it apparently does not need. Most of the government's support under section 3a of the Budget Foundations Law is for education and research, culture and leisure, as well as for religious institutions. On the list of NGOs that receive government support according to Section 3a, there are only 51 organizations classified under the category "Philanthropy and Volunteerism."

**TABLE 6**

**Government support according to Section 3a of the Budget Foundations Law in the distribution to areas of activity (2011)\***

| Field of activity income | Total income (in millions of NIS) | Government support (in millions of NIS) | Number of organizations that receive support |
|---|---|---|---|
| Education and research | 15,771 | 733 | 820 |
| Culture and leisure | 5,717 | 474 | 504 |
| Religion | 3,215 | 410 | 495 |
| Philanthropy | 5,617 | 268 | 51 |
| Welfare | 8,316 | 50 | 130 |
| Environment | 326 | 25 | 35 |
| Civil organizations | 1,144 | 14 | 39 |
| Health | 4,448 | 12 | 55 |
| Housing and development | 648 | 10 | 16 |
| Trade unions | 881 | 4 | 15 |
| Other | 78 | 2 | 7 |
| Total | 46,161 | 2,002 | 2,167 |

*Source: NPTech, Non-profit Organizations in Israel Yearbook, August 2014*

*The data includes government support, according to Section 3a of the Budget Foundations Law only, and it does not include other grants or payment for purchasing services. Also, the data does not include the income of NGOs that are recognized as "public institutions"

In 2012, the NGOs' areas of activity and part of the total non-profit income of the NGOs were as follows: Health, 42.2 percent; Education and research, 28.2 percent; Welfare, 8.9 percent; Culture, entertainment and sports, 7.4 percent; Philanthropy and volunteerism, 5.5 percent; Religion, 3.4 percent; Environment, 0.3 percent; Housing and Development, 0.9 percent; Political and defense organizations, 0.9 percent; International organizations, 0.1 percent and trade unions, 2.2 percent.

Receiving financial support from the government, especially over time, is a long and exhausting process, requiring patience and especially good relations with members of the government and its ministries. The highest aspiration of any social initiative is to build and run a successful model, which provides an effective response to a broad and painful problem and mobilizes the government to adopt and fund this model on a national basis. Nevertheless, mobilizing the government to adopt a non-profit organization model on a national basis is not easy and even unusual in Israel. The Rashi Foundation, headed by Knesset Member and Israel Prize laureate, Mr. Eli Alalouf, excelled in mobilizing the government for social initiatives. One of the best examples of this is the School Lunch Program. The Rashi Foundation played a central role in initiating the National Lunch Program, from the view that providing a nutritious lunch, especially for children from low-income families, is an essential component of programs for extending the school day.

The program was launched in 2004 with the full support of the Rashi Foundation and provided meals for about 1,500 students a day. The foundation first recruited the local councils to participate in the program, and after two years, the foundation succeeded in enlisting the effort of the then minister of education, Rabbi Yitzhak Levy, thereby expanding the program to 5,000 students. About a year later, under the then minister of education, Yossi Sarid, the program expanded to approximately 12,000 children. A few years later, during the Sharon administration, the foundation managed to enlist two Knesset members — Yuli Tamir from the opposition and Ruhama Avraham of the coalition — a competition formed between the opposition and the coalition over the credit for the program. This blessed competition led to Prime Minister Ariel Sharon and his administration adopting the plan on a national basis, and even anchoring it in legislation.

The program expanded, and in 2014, the government allocated 230 million NIS to serve 320,000 meals a day! The Lunch Program is an example of a very successful program that began as an NGO initiative and was fully adopted by the government in legislation. In Eli Alalouf's opinion, the principles of bringing the government into partnership in such initiatives are full and thorough recognition of the political system, patience and hard and informal work with the political system, emphasizing the prestige and status of the outstanding people behind the initiative — in the case of the Rashi Foundation, the prestige and status of the founder of the foundation, Mr. Gustave Leven — as well as taking advantage of political opportunities.

Another example of a social enterprise of a non-profit organization adopted on a national basis is the Karev program. The program was established in 1990 by Andrea and Charles Bronfman, with the goal of promoting social-educational change, reducing gaps and encouraging equal opportunities in Israeli society through enrichment and empowerment activities within the educational system. The enrichment classes of the Karev program are integrated during the school day in schools and kindergartens and are delivered by instructors who are not Ministry of Education employees. The program began in 1990 in two local councils: Jerusalem and Beit Shemesh.

As of today, the program operates in 110 local councils, includes more than 260,000 boys and girls, has become a formal program of the Ministry of Education and is mostly funded by the state. Also in this case, enlisting the government to adopt the Karev program was taking advantage of a rare political opportunity: the great immigration from the former Soviet Union brought with it many professionals and artists, but it created an employment problem, and many of the talented immigrants found themselves unemployed. The adoption of the program on a national basis by the Rabin administration addressed several important issues: extending the school day and exposing Israeli children to new subjects such as music, art, sculpture, theater, etc., and at the same time alleviating the employment problem of some of the immigrants who became employed as counselors in the program.

Few new organizations have succeeded to enlist government support in their first years of activity. In order to attract the attention of the government, organizations need to prove themselves through successful activity on the ground and create demand and pressure from the organization's target audience on the decision-makers. In addition, despite the strong desire to receive government assistance, it is important to emphasize that government aid that is not anchored in long-term and approved agreements at the highest levels has the potential for instability, and it is very difficult to rely on it. Any political change in the composition of the government or the minister in charge may drastically change the level of government support for the organization. Therefore, such support is very desirable, but it is important not to rely exclusively on it unless the responsibility for the organization's activities is adopted and anchored in government decisions.

# 3.

## THE SCOPE OF DONATIONS FROM ISRAEL

As mentioned above, almost every social initiative, especially a social initiative falling under the definition of "philanthropy and volunteerism," will depend mainly on its ability to raise resources, meaning, the organization's ability to raise funds. Most start-up organizations rely on private donors or institutions from Israel and abroad at least in their initial years of activity. The strong desire to begin activity immediately after securing limited financial support becomes an obstacle that leads many organizations to a serious crisis, and even to a cessation of activity shortly after it begins. Therefore, one of the most important things to thoroughly think about prior to embarking on a social initiative is the financial sustainability of the organization over the years; it is important to understand how the organization intends to raise financial support to sustain itself over time. Although a clear and professional plan for raising resources for the organization is not a guarantee of success, it certainly reduces risks and increases the chances of the initiative's success.

Monetary donations to Israeli non-profit organizations are received from Israel and abroad. Israeli philanthropy includes donations to nonprofits from households, companies and estates in Israel. Most of the donations, both from Israel and abroad, are given to philanthropy and volunteerism (23 percent of donations are from Israel and 48 percent are from abroad), education and research (22 percent and 13 percent, respectively). However, the areas that rely mainly on donations are international organizations (donations from Israel and abroad constitute 85 percent of revenues), advocacy and politics (68 percent) and philanthropy and volunteerism (60 percent). In the other fields, the total income from donations does not exceed 48 percent, and the area in which this is the lowest is the area of health: donations make up only three percent of the income.[21]

### TABLE 7

### Israeli philanthropy and philanthropy from abroad, by year
*(in millions of shekels)*

| Year | Total donations | Donations from Israel to NGOs | Donations from abroad to NGOs | Donations from abroad to national institutions |
|------|-----------------|-------------------------------|-------------------------------|-----------------------------------------------|
| 2009 | 12,799 | 4,700 | 7,327 | 772 |
| 2010 | 12,845 | 4,964 | 6,807 | 1,074 |
| 2011 | 14,756 | 5,680 | 8,056 | 1,020 |

*Source: "Committed to Give" survey and the Central Bureau of Statistics, 2014*

As mentioned above, the main income of NGOs is from government transfers, sale of services and transfers from the private sector. Transfers from the private sector include "in goods," which are transfers of goods and services equivalent to money, transfers from other NGOs, philanthropy from abroad and Israeli philanthropy. It's hard to estimate the precise scope of the monetary donations of Israelis to non-profit organizations in Israel since only about 22 percent of the donations from Israelis — households, companies and estates — are reported for tax credit purposes. An average of 44 percent of the donations that come from companies is reported for tax credit purposes, compared to 15 percent of the donations coming from households. In Israel, NGO income from estates stands at less than 2.5 percent of all donations from Israel, compared with nine percent in the United States. A survey conducted by the Central Bureau of Statistics in cooperation with the Committed to Give organization and the Yad Hanadiv foundation on Israeli philanthropy between 2009 and 2011 showed that the scope of donations from businesses and households among Israelis increased from 4.7 billion NIS in 2009 to 5.7 billion NIS in 2011 — an impressive increase of 21 percent. This survey also showed that financial donations from Israelis account for about 40 percent of all financial donations to NGOs from Israel and abroad, not including donations from abroad to national institutions: the Jewish Agency, the Jewish National Fund and Keren Hayesod - United Israel Appeal.[22]

## TABLE 8

### Israeli donations according to source
*(in millions of shekels)*

| Year | Total donations, | From companies | From households | From estates |
|------|------------------|----------------|-----------------|--------------|
| 2009 | 4,700 | 1,318 | 3,225 | 157 |
| 2010 | 4,964 | 1,250 | 3,628 | 86 |
| 2011 | 5,680 | 1,554 | 4,026 | 100 |

*Source: The Central Bureau of Statistics*

In Israel, as in the United States, most donations are made by the general public. More than 65 percent of total donations from Israelis to non-profit organizations are received from households; compared to 71 percent, out of total donations of $373.25 billion, in the United States. In addition, the vast majority of total donations received from households — 91 percent — are donations of sums below 100,000 NIS. A survey conducted by the Institute of Law and Philanthropy at Tel Aviv University on patterns of giving of households in Israel in 2016 showed that 76 percent of Israelis donate money or money equivalent. The average annual donation per household stands at only 300 NIS, one of the lowest in Western countries. Only about 15 percent of the respondents donated more than 1,000 shekels a year, and 2.3 percent donated more than 10,000 a year.[23]

By comparison, in 2015, the average per capita contribution in the United States was $1,000 per person. On the other hand, about 27 percent of Israeli donations to NGOs are donations from Israeli companies. Many of the donations received from companies — 40-45 percent — are at a high amount of 500,000 NIS. The average contribution range for donor companies under 100,000 NIS ranges from 20,000 NIS to 38,000 NIS.[24] These facts highlight the relative lack of involvement of companies and wealthy people in social action in Israel. The economic success of companies and the huge increase in the number of wealthy people in recent years are not reflected in the donation curve in Israel. According to Credit Suisse's Global Wealth Report for 2016, the number of millionaires in Israel whose estimated capital is between one million and five million dollars is 91,000, between five and ten million dollars is 8,000, between 10 million and 15 million dollars is 5,000, between 50 million and 100 million dollars is 444, between 100 million and 500 million dollars is 277, between 500 million and one billion is 25, and there are 18 Israeli billionaires with capital estimated at more than one billion dollars.[25] These facts indicate the widening gap between the ability to give and actual giving in Israel.

The negative attitude toward the third sector and the fear of some of the wealthy people to be exposed can explain some of this grim picture. But the changes in the donation habits of Diaspora Jewry, the accumulated wealth and the ever-growing demands of non-profit organizations in Israel certainly necessitate a fundamental change in the donation habits and the growing involvement of wealthy people and companies in social action in Israel. This understanding led to the establishment of two of the most important bodies for promoting philanthropy in Israel: Committed to Give and the Jewish Funders Network (JFN Israel).

The Committed to Give initiative works to expand the circle of donors in Israel and to cultivate the next generation of Israeli philanthropy. It does so by changing the culture of giving among the financially capable in Israel, by promoting and cultivating significant Israeli philanthropy and by encouraging and motivating for strategic and effective giving. This initiative consists of a group of Israeli donors who chose to work together to encourage personal involvement and financial contribution from personal capital for social purposes. The initiative works to change perceptions and to increase the number of significant givers in Israel. The Israeli Jewish Funder Network (JFN Israel) was established in order to enable Israeli donors and capital owners to exchange ideas about their philanthropic involvement and to expand the circles of giving in which they are a part of, both in Israel and overseas. In addition, JFN Israel serves as a mediator for philanthropists from abroad who wish to enter the circles of social influence in Israel and expand their philanthropic activity in Israel.

The understanding and internalization that the vast majority of donations to NGOs come from private individuals are very important for non-profit organizations when making a fundraising plan. Most organizations seek donations from institutions, foundations and especially rich people, but the fact is that most of the donations come from the general public. Non-profit organizations based on donations from the general public rely on slightly more stable ground than those that rely on support from institutions and government ministries. The changes in support from the general public are slow, as opposed to the shock of the cessation of a donor's contribution, such as a government ministry. The problem with small donations from private individuals is that they are scattered and inconsistent, and require serious and constant maintenance. Another problem is that many of them are one-time donations. And it is easier to renew donations in small amounts than in large sums. The vast majority of donations today are received through traditional recruitment methods such as personal meetings, phone calls, direct mail and e-mail.

Even in the age of the Internet and social networks, the ways in which Israelis give have not significantly changed: 58 percent donate to beggars on the street, 57 percent through door-to-door operations, 52 percent in charity boxes, 50 percent in supermarkets and 4.2 percent via text messages. Of the total donations made by Israelis to NGOs in 2016, only 7.5 percent were made via the Internet.[26] In comparison, in the United States in 2015, about 7.1 percent of total donations of 373.25 billion dollars were received via the Internet. Although the amount of donations via the Internet in the United States constitutes a small portion of total donations, this reflects a nine percent increase from the previous year, an increase indicating a growing trend.[27]

In the virtual world in which we live, organizations must think about recruiting social networks as a means of connecting with the general public and making the organization's message accessible to as many people as possible. This is not a simple challenge, since the motive to donate for a large part of the donors is emotional, while some simply feel uncomfortable in the face of the person who asks them and they agree. The sense of identity and sense of belonging usually compensate for the virtual barriers to donation. Evidence of this is the great success in raising funds for political purposes, such as the online fundraising of former US President Barack Obama. Therefore, an organization's ability to convey the sense of partnership and personal influence and make the donation part of the identity of the virtual donor in social networks is the key to success in enlisting masses over time. Another challenge in fundraising on social networks is organizations' ability to organize large groups of small private donors and to keep them for long periods of time. Maintaining continuous contact by updating affiliates and full transparency of what is happening with their money, raises the chances of a recurring donation from the same source. Advanced fundraising methods such as "donation days," challenge gifts and fundraising through social networks can provide an opportunity to meet with potential donors. But it is always important to remember that every fundraising effort must be accompanied by a strategy to identify and retain appropriate donors and to enlist these donors for long-term giving. Research on donor habits in the United States shows that between 50 and 60 percent of an organization's donors donate to it only once. In addition, the cost of obtaining a new donor is five times greater than the cost of retaining an existing donor.[28] In 2015, the rate of retention of customers or donors in the United States was 46 percent. In other words, only 46 percent of the donors from 2014 made a recurring donation the following year.[29] With a fixed and even shrinking pool of donors, recruiting new donors has become harder and more expensive than ever. In addition, since 60 percent of donors drop out after one donation, sometimes the cost of recruiting the donor exceeds the donor's contribution. Therefore, most of the effort in fundraising in recent years has focused on retaining customers or donors.[30] An intelligent investment in interpersonal relationships in the effort to fundraise can result in donation growth and the retention of donors over time.

As we have seen, the strength of an NGO or non-profit organization is dependent on the recruitment of quality donors, especially those who make donations over time rather than on a one-time basis. In what other ways can this be done? Another way to recruit and retain donors is through fundraising events. These events are meant to create a positive impression, deepen relationships with donors and build relationships with potential donors. Of course, the atmosphere of the fundraising event should match the organization's message. A grandiose fundraising event for an organization that works for the sake of the weak and the needy will miss the message. The event is supposed to convey credibility, professionalism and prestige, and create a sense of belonging between the donors and the organization. Donors and guests — the potential donors — should receive personal attention and feel that they have received a worthy value for their donation. Yet, organizing a fundraising event is not a trivial matter and requires detailed planning. The production of an event requires effort, maximum attention from the organization's management and cooperation between all branches of the organization: fundraising, marketing, public relations, logistics and more.

Beyond the income, strengthening the bond with the donors and creating the initial connection with potential donors, a successful fundraising event raises public awareness of the organization's activities, raises the morale of the organization's employees and expands its circles of influence. Therefore, one can say that the most important thing in fundraising is to generate credibility with the potential donor. The donors are clever and intelligent people, and they can sense us and that which is truly driving us in our social action. You cannot create fake credibility over time. When the issue we are promoting is burning in our bones, when we come with a pure motive, when we believe with all our hearts in the objective that we are promoting — we emanate credibility and infectious enthusiasm. In such a situation, it is hard to stand on the side and not join in.

Such an enormous effort made the members of the board of directors of Ofanim enter into a healthy competition for getting additional donations, in the aspect of "writer's envy increases wisdom." The involvement of the members of the board of directors in the effort to raise donations deepened both the personal commitment and the sense of "ownership" and responsibility for the organization. Indeed, during the 14 years of its existence, Ofanim has managed to raise tens of millions of shekels in Israel, more than half of its annual budget. This is a tremendous achievement that few non-profit organizations in Israel can be proud of. And as a reminder, this was also one of the goals of the organization when it was established. Success has many fathers, but it also has mothers; one of the main reasons for Ofanim's success and its achievement in fundraising in Israel lies in the woman who led this effort: Poly Meschiany, the first employee of Ofanim.

Poly believed in the idea of the organization and was so enthusiastic about it that she decided to join the organization in return for a symbolic salary. Before joining Ofanim, she had never raised any donations. But the integrity, the credibility, the professionalism and the modesty that emanated from her broke through barriers and penetrated the hearts of donors. Poly's enthusiasm and total identification with the organization's goals infected many others and made them want to join in the effort. For seven years, Poly led the effort and built the organization's fundraising infrastructure. Poly then became CEO of Ofanim for another three years. It is hard to overstate her essential and important contribution, and it is for that reason everyone calls her "the mother of Ofanim."

# CHAPTER SIX:

# ADDITIONAL SOURCES
# OF INCOME

*There is no wealth like health, and no pleasantness like a good heart.*

- Rabbi Shlomo Ibn Gabirol

# 1.

## DONATIONS FROM BUSINESSES
## AND COMPANIES

Another very important source of fundraising is from businesses and companies. In the not-so-distant past, social responsibility was placed primarily on state authorities and non-profit organizations. Businesses, on the other hand, were focused almost exclusively on the economic field. Until recently, "Corporate social responsibility" befitted the statement of the economist, Milton Friedman: "There is one and only one responsibility of a business— the responsibility to use its resources and engage in business activities in order to maximize its profits so long as it stays within the rules of the game".[1]

The change in the corporate responsibility approach took place at the United Nations Conference on Environment and Development, held in Rio de Janeiro, Brazil in 1992, and for the first time, representatives of the business sector participated. At this conference, the initial foundations were laid for the expectation of multinational and local corporations to voluntarily report on their social and environmental impact. In July 2001, the European Commission established that corporate responsibility was founded on a voluntary basis. This voluntary approach gave corporations a free hand in choosing the appropriate scope of social corporate responsibility for their business and competitive considerations.[2] Corporations operating in accordance with the voluntary approach see their social activities as charitable and philanthropic. They assume that in the allocation of a certain annual amount destined for donations to the public, they're operating with full social responsibility. A more progressive perception of social responsibility holds that true social responsibility is not a matter of altruism and good-heartedness but must be linked to the core business of the corporate activity. This approach is based on the perception that corporations must take into account the social, environmental and economic impact of their activities at the early stage of product development and service provision.[3]

In recent years, the social responsibility of companies and businesses has gone from a concept that represents ideology and a voluntary perception to a necessary reality that is expected of business organizations. The assumption is that by demonstrating social responsibility on the part of companies and businesses, they are capable of creating a better world and that alongside their commitment to shareholder profitability, they must also manage and safeguard the interests of other stakeholders such as employees, suppliers, consumers, the community and the environment.[4] The call for corporate social responsibility is a call for norms of behavior that are more obligatory than the law imposes on corporations — moral norms that deviate from the corporation's perception as a profit and loss unit.[5] This call was answered by the

European Union in December 2014, with the approval of a new policy — Directive EU / 2014/95. As of 2017, this policy obligates approximately 6,000 corporations — such as public companies, banks and insurance companies that employ more than 500 employees and will be defined as public interest entities — to report annually on their activities and their environmental and social impact.

Toward the end of the 1990s, two legislative updates relating to the social activities of the Israeli corporations were made in Israel, which encouraged corporate social responsibility. The first is an update of the section "Purpose of the Company" in the Companies Law, 5759-1999. This update allows businesses to donate to worthy social causes, even in cases where the donation is not part of business considerations. This update gives legal authorization for corporate philanthropy and encourages donations. Another step to encourage and institutionalize philanthropy was the amendment to the Securities Regulations that was enacted in 2001, which determined that Israeli public corporations must also add a description of the extent of their donations to the reports included in their financial statements.[6] However, these legislative updates left corporate social responsibility in Israel in the voluntary realm and in the sole discretion of the business companies. In the past, a bill was drafted calling on Israeli companies to submit an annual corporate responsibility report, but the proposal was not passed. Today, there is no obligation to file a corporate responsibility report in Israel, and as far as I know, the matter is not even on the Knesset's agenda.[7] This is why in Israel a very small number of corporations publish their social activities in their financial reports. In 2015, for example, 20 corporate responsibility reports were published in Israel. This is a 30 percent decline in the number of publications compared to 2014, when 28 corporate responsibility reports were published, yet this is a small increase compared to 2013, when 18 reports were published.[8]

Nevertheless, due to the political and social changes that the Israeli economy has undergone in recent years, there has been a shift in the perception of part of the business community regarding social responsibility. The processes of privatization, liberalization, deregulation and globalization, the shrinking of the welfare state and the rise of inequality have all led to diverting the attention of civil society organizations and social activists to the social activities of business corporations and to the increasing demand for the expansion of the social obligations that have been placed on them.[9]

One of the most important infrastructure organizations established in Israel is Maala, an organization that has been active since 1998 to increase the awareness of the business sector of the importance of corporate responsibility in the general social fabric. Maala is an umbrella organization of about 110 leading companies in the Israeli economy, which promotes corporate responsibility and the development of responsible administration standards in Israel. With the objective of raising awareness of corporate responsibility in Israel, Maala established the Annual Corporate Responsibility Conference, a socio-economic arena for business leaders, decision-makers from the public sector and heads of social and environmental organizations. The organization also founded the "Maala Index" for corporate responsibility, along with the Corporate Responsibility Management training course that established the corporate responsibility management profession in Israel. The "Maala Index" enables annual evaluation, mapping of gaps and setting goals for improvement, in relation to the standards and norms in Israel. The criteria in the rankings are determined by an independent public committee composed of content experts, academics, heads of social and environmental organizations and representatives of the business sector.[10]

In recent years, donations from Israeli businesses and companies accounted for 27 percent of the total Israeli donations to NGOs in Israel. In the United States, on the other hand, the total amount of corporate donations account for 5 percent of total donations to NGOs. The reason that the percentage of donations to NGOs is higher in Israel than in the United States is that the culture of foundations in Israel — family, private and corporate — is still in its infancy. Therefore, a large number of Israeli business people donate their donations through their companies. In the United States, on the other hand, where the culture of foundations is highly developed, many business people establish foundations and donate through them. Therefore, about 16 percent of total donations to NGOs in the United States come from foundations, compared with the fraction of the percentage obtained from the few foundations in Israel. Another way to look at the overall donation of businesses and foundations to

NGOs is in relation to GDP: in 2014, the amount of donations received from businesses and foundations for NGOs in Israel — approximately 1.7 billion NIS — constituted about .019 percent of the GDP in Israel. This is compared to the amount of donations from businesses and foundations for NGOs in the United States — approximately 76 billion dollars — which constitutes about 0.43 percent of the GDP in the United States. Central Bureau of Statistics data on the scope of Israeli donations to NGOs shows a dismal picture of the extent of the donation of Israeli companies; the vast majority of donations to NGOs come from households in Israel and donations from abroad.[11] This is especially surprising in light of the economic growth and Israel's flourishing high-tech industry, which has created a new generation of young wealthy people who can make a social impact. The lack of devotion of Israeli companies to social action for the sake of the weak and needy in society, from whom they generate huge profits, is inappropriate behavior. The reality in which companies' profits are skyrocketing, yet they are still turning a cold shoulder to society, is a reality that cannot last for long.

We already noted that, although there is no obligation to report corporate social activity in Israel, some companies allocate an amount of their profits each year to support the social activities of non-profit organizations. The corporate social responsibility of most companies in Israel is not strategic — it is a matter of giving to charity and philanthropy. Many see their social responsibility as part of their public relations. It is important for these companies that their social contribution receives a public response. Companies often place conditions on their donations that conflict with the principal objectives of the organization they seek to donate to. However, despite the great temptation to accept the donation, it is very important to be loyal to the vision of the non-profit organization and its objectives.

In 2015, one of Israel's leading companies chose Ofanim as its flagship organization and offered to support the organization with a donation of one million shekels each year for ten years. Donations of this kind of sum are very rare in Israel. This is a donation that could constitute a serious financial anchor and save a lot of effort in fundraising. The organization established a team headed by the CEO in order to manage negotiations with the company regarding the conditions for the donation. We were very disappointed when the company insisted that as a condition of its donation, Ofanim had to change the basic activity model — a model that worked with the same groups of children every week and accompanied them over the years, which was something that limited the number of children exposed to the organization's activities but deepened the impact on the children. The company insisted on changing the activity model so that the organization would come to new groups of children each week for one-time meetings so that it would be possible to present a very high number of children that the organization "impacts" with the help of the company's donation. Our claims that one-time exposure meetings are ineffective and that the chances of making a deep and genuine impact require long-term guidance for these children had fallen on deaf ears. The company saw only the ability to leverage the donation as part of its public relations campaign and not the wellbeing of the children for whom the organization was founded. In order to remain loyal to the organization's objectives, we were forced to refuse the company and forgo the rare multi-year donation.

As mentioned, few companies see their social responsibility as part of their business core. Many of the donor companies also require the involvement of their employees as volunteers in the work of the non-profit organizations that they donate to. Many of them set this as a pre-requisite for their donation. Although the intention behind this demand is good and positive, this condition sometimes constitutes an obstacle for non-profit organizations operating in areas that are far from the location of the company's offices, as well as for non-profit organizations whose activities are carried out by professional workers and not by volunteers.

The chances that a new non-profit organization will receive a donation from a large company in Israel are very slim, unless the organization has connections with the decision makers in the company. The greater the visibility of the non-profit organization, the easier it will be to get the attention of the donor companies. The intensive activity of the members of the board of directors of Ofanim in opening doors to senior executives in the Israeli economy has earned it support from a large portion of the largest and most well-known companies in the Israeli economy. The greater the visibility of Ofanim, the more willing companies are to donate to it. In general, it is easier for companies to donate to high-visibility non-profit organizations. As a result, most large companies "adopt" one organization with high visibility, to whom they provide the lion's share of their donations, while the rest are divided among several non-profit organizations. For example, in 2014, the total donations of Bank Leumi, one of the leading and most profitable banks in Israel, amounted to approximately 30 million NIS, which constituted 1.07 percent of the bank's pre-tax profits that year — for sponsorships and community social objectives. The donation was distributed among 230 organizations, and 12 million NIS was donated to Aharai, the flagship non-profit organization of the bank.

The fact that most donor companies do not strategically see their social responsibility, leads to these companies switching their support for non-profit organizations every few years. This creates instability in non-profit organizations and sends them to find new sources of funding each year. The ability to choose a small number of non-profit organizations that represent the values of the company and cooperate with them over time is the most appropriate and beneficial way — both for the non-profit organization and the donor company. For the non-profit organization, a long-term commitment is an anchor and provides financial stability. For the company, a long-term commitment is an opportunity to become deeply acquainted with the activities of the non-profit organization, to influence it and be a significant part of its life.

# 2.

## MATCHING FUNDING

In the last decade, there has been a significant change in the issue of fundraising for social initiatives in Israel. In the past, many non-profit organizations could rely mainly on donations from abroad. Today, organizations and donors from abroad have become more inquisitive and meticulous, seeking partnerships with Israelis mainly in philanthropic ventures. The concept of "matching" — a partnership in financial support from Israel and abroad — has become common and in many cases, is a pre-requisite for receiving donations from abroad. These support partnerships have many advantages for both the donors and the non-profit organizations. Given the vast amount of capital that Israel has accumulated in recent decades, the idea that an initiative seeking to bring about social change in Israel will be based solely on donor funds from abroad, without a serious effort to recruit Israeli donors, is not only insulting but also inappropriate. The involvement of Israelis in financing a local social initiative is, first and foremost, a manifestation of solidarity and social responsibility, and a testimony to the importance and necessity of the initiative. In addition, the involvement of local donors in social projects adds a level of control over the conduct of the initiative. Understanding the culture and orientation in the depths of Israeli society helps the local donors closely monitor the management of the initiative. On the other hand, overseas donors, who occasionally visit Israel and are unfamiliar with Israeli culture, find it more difficult to monitor the management of the initiative. Moreover, donors from abroad feel that the request for support from Israeli social initiatives that are also based on donations from Israel is done with clean hands.

Partnership in financial support also leads to partnership in setting the goals and objectives of the social initiatives and leads to healthier relationships between donors and social entrepreneurs. This change in the concept of fundraising, which requires that the social initiatives make an effort to achieve donations in Israel, is a welcome change because it indirectly helps for more effective management of non-profit organizations, strengthens solidarity in Israel and increases social involvement by recruiting more Israelis into the circle of social action.

In Ofanim we set two main goals for ourselves: one is empowering and promoting the children of the remote socio-economically weak locations in Israel, the second is creating circles of solidarity and social involvement. For us, both goals were of equal importance. To achieve the second goal, we set ourselves a target that in retrospect seemed very ambitious: financing the project in complete partnership between donors from Israel and donors from abroad — meaning, 50 percent funding from Israel and 50 percent financing from abroad. In order to show the importance that we see in this objective and the seriousness with which we relate to achieving it, we placed it in a central place in the organization's documents and have instilled it in the organizational culture of Ofanim. Every employee and donor, and basically anyone who comes into contact with Ofanim, knows that this is a central objective of the organization. The implementation of this important objective has positive side results, and they are also the underlying idea of partnership in support. Achieving funding from Israelis is an effort that requires very serious fieldwork, thereby creating new ripples of social solidarity and responsibility.

Only those who have experience fundraising in Israel know how difficult and almost impossible the goal we set for ourselves is. There is no doubt that we have displayed tremendous naivete in our approach to fundraising in Israel, but it seems that sometimes we must be a bit naïve in order to set very high goals. The fact that half of the organization's budget must come from Israeli sources forced us to think of a thorough and detailed plan to raise funds in Israel. In addition, the rate of expansion of the organization, especially at the beginning, was a result of our ability to raise local funds. The significance of this mission — to get many more Israelis to be involved in an educational initiative for the children of the remote locations — excited us and pushed us to achieve it. The absolute commitment of the members of the board of directors of Ofanim to achieving this objective is an example of a total commitment and devotion to the mission. Beyond achieving the ambitious target set by Ofanim — raising half of the budget from Israeli sources — its achievement, in my humble opinion, of course, is mainly in the success of bringing many more Israelis into the circle of giving and social action in Israel.

Personal connections are the key to success in a fundraising effort. Like closing a deal in the business world, a donation in the social sector also depends on personal relations and trust between the parties. Almost all the big donors point out the paramount importance they place on their level of trust toward the leaders of the non-profit organization. Donations to large institutions, in particular, usually involve a basic personal connection between the institution and the donor: it is reasonable to assume that the donor or a member of his family attended the particular university, was hospitalized in the same hospital or was present at an exhibition in the museum, for example. The leading professional staff at these large institutions is trained and highly skilled in converting such personal connections into large donations. Therefore, reaching a potential donor, private or institutional, through a personal contact drastically increases the chances of receiving a donation.

On the other hand, in small or mid-sized social initiatives, especially those defined as "philanthropy and volunteerism," there may be a connection between the donor and the subject that the initiatives seek to promote — for example, feeding hungry people, protecting wildlife or advancing children in education.[12] In such social initiatives, the vision and idea of the non-profit organization and the connections and the persuasiveness of its leaders are important factors for success in the fundraising effort. The fact that Ofanim is one of the few organizations that provides educational enrichment in science to the children of small and remote locations, using innovative and attractive means, has helped open the hearts and pockets of many Israeli donors.

A large portion of the non-profit organizations in Israel approach the well-known wealthy people in Israel: about 15 to 20 of the wealthiest families who donate on a regular basis. The large amount of requests for donations received by these families leaves very little chance for new requests from new non-profit organizations. In addition, almost all wealthy families are identified with a non-profit organization that they give the lion's share of their annual donation to, which leaves little opportunity for new non-profit organizations to receive any sort of donation. Ofanim concentrated on recruiting young businessmen, mainly from high-tech, who made a medium-sized fortune. These businessmen are not in the sights of many non-profit organizations, and the competition for their donations is less difficult. These young businessmen could easily relate and connect to the scientific-technological message of Ofanim and brought new ideas and energies to the organization, and mainly recruited some of their friends as donors. Achieving these donors required enormous effort, and time. The effort of the board members to open the doors of organizations, institutions and private donors to the fundraising team was critical.

People do not donate to institutions, rather to people — especially to people they believe in and in their motives. Therefore, the fundraising process begins with "Friend Raising" and getting to know people requires time and investment. The more familiar and close you are, the greater the chance of support. Many of the Ofanim supporters from the United States became close friends of mine and my family — much thanks to my wife and my family's total commitment to the effort. Our home is wide open and regularly hosts most of the friends — donors of Ofanim. During the summer, when many of the Ofanim supporters visit Israel, sometimes with their families, our home becomes a regular meeting place, especially on Shabbat evenings. These personal encounters, in a warm and loving family atmosphere, constitute a fertile ground for the formation of true friendships, friendships based on shared values that see importance in social action, and totally identify with the objectives of the non-profit organization. To a large extent, Ofanim became a link between me and many of my best friends today.

The tremendous effort invested by the board of directors and the professional staff of Ofanim in Israel spurred the US friends of Ofanim to deepen their commitment. They recognized that when we asked them to open their hearts and their pockets, we came with clean hands. They felt like true partners in the effort of Ofanim to change the face of Israeli society, even if it is in the slightest bit.

# 3.

## CREATING ANCHORS

In addition to raising funds from young business people, we looked at ways to create economic anchors in the organization's fundraising. The idea of creating anchors is to build an infrastructure of regular and long-term donations. The Sisyphean race that happens every year to raise 50 percent of the budget in Israel is exhausting and becomes more difficult each year. Every non-profit organization must think about ways to find economic anchors that are appropriate for it and its activities.

After three years of activity in remote communities and receiving very positive feedback from the regional councils within which the organization operated, as well as from the parents of the children who participated in the activity, we decided to try to do something bold and ask the regional councils to participate in partial funding of Ofanim activities in their areas. This was not an easy decision to make because we knew that participation in funding was not simple for most of these regional councils, most of which are classified in a low socio-economic cluster. The decision was made for two reasons: the first was the high demand for Ofanim activities by many regional councils that asked us to expand our activities into their areas. This, of course, was important feedback for us and gave us confidence that the service we are providing is important and sought after. However, we wanted to check and make sure that the great demand was not coming only because our activity is fully subsidized. We wanted to see whether our activity was important enough to them that they would agree to participate, even in a small part, in the funding. The second reason was to create a financial anchor; agreement to participate in part of the costs of the activities would constitute a fixed income and would reduce the annual fundraising burden.

And so, in light of the good relations we generated with the heads of the regional councils, we began a round of talks in order to recruit them to this process. At first, we asked for participation in funding of five percent of the overall cost of the activities. To our joy and surprise, we did not encounter any great difficulties, and we received agreement from all the regional councils in which we operated to participate in funding the activities. Moreover, the great demand for the organization's activities remained as it was and even increased, despite the request for participation in funding the activities. In light of this, over the years we have raised the demand for funding coming from the regional councils from five percent to close to 20 percent of the costs of the activities. Beyond giving validation to the necessity of the activities of Ofanim, the participation of the regional councils in financing the activities constituted a serious anchor for us in raising funds and reduced the burden of our fundraising. After we succeeded in building this support anchor, we looked for additional anchors to further reduce the difficult burden of raising money in Israel. Other anchors that we succeeded in creating — with much success — include the commitment of every member of the board of directors to achieve — get or give — 50,000 NIS a year and the establishment of Friends of Ofanim in Israel, in which the members pledge to donate 1,000 NIS a year for five years. Obtaining anchors of financial support for non-profit organizations is not easy; it requires serious consideration and the investment of a huge, ongoing effort, but obtaining them makes for a stable financial infrastructure.

As was noted above, one of the problems of donors such as institutions, foundations and individuals in Israel is the desire to distribute their donations among as many non-profit organizations as possible. Therefore, most donors do not donate to the same non-profit organization over time, and every few years they choose other non-profit organizations to donate to. More than once when we returned to receive a donation, the answer we got was, "Last year I donated to you, this year I will donate to a different non-profit organization." This approach leads to financial instability for many non-profit organizations and forces them to newly deal every year with finding new sources of funding. In addition to the fact that the number of sources of funding in Israel is limited, this phenomenon creates financial difficulties for many non-profit organizations and often causes them to shut down their activities. Donors like institutions, foundations and individuals must find strategic partners and support them over time until they can build a strong and steady alternative financing infrastructure.

Motivated leadership and a high sense of a social mission, as well as a well-developed social infrastructure to support donors and potential donors, lead to a greater number of donors and significantly increased donations. The perfect example of social leadership for me and one of the most wonderful gifts I have received as a result of my social involvement is the acquaintance with Mr. Paul Silberberg. Paul is a world leader of Jewish philanthropy in the United States. He is a special person, imbued with a sense of mission, whose entire being speaks social action for the sake of the other — a true "mensch" and Zionist in his soul. We met for the first time in early 1999, when both of us helped the founder of Home Depot, Mr. Bernie Marcus, promote the Israel Democracy Institute, which he supported. I had never before met such a decent, ethical, professional and friendly man who was so imbued with a sense of mission like Paul.

Paul is one of the earliest principals of CMS Companies and was president of the company for about 40 years. At its peak, the company employed 120 employees, and during the course of its activities, it acquired approximately 12 billion dollars in properties and approximately six billion dollars in life insurance. The company focused on building relationships with successful entrepreneurs. Beyond being a particularly successful company in its field, its uniqueness lies in its deep social commitment. According to CMS's perspective, the world consists of two types of people: miners and farmers. Miners take from the world, while farmers take but also give back to the world. CMS has chosen its customers, partners and employees with piety — only those who are farmers in their nature. All of the company's employees are involved in social action. Paul himself was a member of the board of directors of Friends of Yemin Orde, and through his encouragement, I also joined its board of directors in the United States.

When I returned to Israel, I joined the Yemin Orde Youth Village's board of directors, and I later served for three years as chairman of Yemin Orde Educational Initiatives. Paul led the fundraising campaign for the youth village from 1999 to 2008. During those years, Paul successfully raised 80 million dollars in funds for the youth village. Paul's leadership set a personal example; before turning to donors, he himself would donate generously. He opened his heart, enlisted his home and his family and gave his money for the purpose he believed in.

I often went to join Paul in a fund-raising campaign, and every time I came out thrilled by his ability to get people to identify with the objective that he promoted. Paul's charm was expressed in the reliability he conveyed and his total commitment to the cause. The pleasant, friendly and professional way in which he approached the donors, along with the credibility and integrity that emanated from him, turned the donors into his good friends, and they wanted with all their might to be his partners in social action. It's no wonder, then, that the first person I approached when we founded Ofanim was Paul. I asked him for his help and advice. Paul was enthusiastic about the idea and promised to enlist his partners at CMS to finance one of the first busses of Ofanim. In addition, Paul agreed to my request to join the board of directors of Friends of Ofanim in the United States, which had been established several months before that. Him joining gave a tremendous boost to the organization and gave me and the members of the administration of Ofanim in Israel great confidence. My joy over Paul joining was twofold; beyond the tremendous power that it added to the organization, I was glad that my connection with this amazing man would be on a regular basis, even after I returned to Israel.

During the initial years after I returned to Israel, we were both members of the boards of directors of Yemin Orde and Ofanim. In 2008, when Paul successfully completed his fundraising campaign and achieved the incredible target of raising 80 million dollars, he decided to retire from the board of directors of Friends of Yemin Orde in the United States. After his retirement, Paul received many offers to lead various social initiatives in the United States. On one of our shared vacations, I took advantage of the opportunity, and as we hung between the heavens and the earth in a cable car at a ski resort in Colorado, I pleaded with him to take on the position of chairman of the Friends of Ofanim in the United States. Paul was surprised at first, but after repeated pleading, I managed to get him to agree, and that's how I knew the success of Ofanim was guaranteed. As part of my gentlemanly agreement with Paul, I committed myself to at least two annual visits, each for one a week, to help with the fundraising effort of Friends of Ofanim in the United States.

Working with Paul was an instructive lesson for me in several ways. In my professional life, I worked with a large number of highly professional people, but I never saw a person who was as thorough and professional as Paul. The consideration of fine details of each thing and the careful preparation before each meeting left nothing to chance. His absolute commitment and tremendous investment simply left me feeling thrilled. He enlisted his entire family, his company and its employees, as well as all of his friends. The packed schedule of meetings started at 7:00 a.m. and often ended after midnight. We would scan the United States, far and wide, around the clock. Every time I returned from my visit to the United States, I was exhausted from the effort but satisfied with the privilege of having been with him.

Paul personally knows many of the leading business people in the United States, which is something that is very rare. It was amazing to see that wherever we went, people were happy to meet Paul, even though they knew the purpose of his visit. The grace, the pleasantness and the mischievousness with which he presented the organization's message, together with the tremendous commitment and absolute trust he conveyed, left his interlocutors with no option but to join the effort. In his special way, Paul also spurred and triggered the other board members of Friends of Ofanim to help expand the circle of donors. Paul's connection with the donors, most of whom were also his friends, was constant and continuous. The way he worked to maintain this connection is something that should be taught in schools. He wrote down every detail of every meeting. He gave out tasks and kept track of them until they were completed. Not one day passed that I did not receive dozens of emails from him about Ofanim. As far as he was concerned, the fundraising targets that had been set by the board of directors were sacred, and everything had to be done in order to achieve them. In the seven years that Paul was the chairman of Friends of the Ofanim in the United States, we never missed our fundraising targets in the United States. In addition to this, Ofanim also enjoyed the donation made by his generous family each year.

To this day I cannot understand how he managed to do so much in addition to managing his own company and raising his family. His interest and concern for the children of Ofanim was deep and sincere — as far as he was concerned, they were all his children. The vast majority of the many Ofanim children did not get to know him personally, but I always knew they were lucky to have him taking care of them. Beyond the amazing lessons I learned from him, the time I spent with him contributed to the development of a deep and unique friendship. He became a big brother to me — a brother by choice.

In the book that Paul wrote, The Ethical Entrepreneur: Succeeding in Business without Selling Your Soul, he reveals his "Ten Commandments" for a fundraising campaign.[13] Paul qualifies and writes that these rules are not engraved in stone and that each person should adapt them to his needs. I was lucky enough to have witnessed the implementation of these rules and I saw how effective they are, and therefore I am presenting them here:

1. Define your mission clearly. There are always competing missions and pressures from different directions: do not blur the message.

2. Remember that people give to people. People respond in times of crisis or distress, people respond to opportunities, and most importantly, people respond to people.

3. Define your impact. We all want to influence and leave a mark. Promote a glorious vision that calls for real change.

4. Go public with your goal. Set goals that are achievable but high. A big dream. It is not the amount of money that counts, but rather what it is that you want to achieve.

5. Assign bite-size tasks on the way to achieving the goal. Divide your goal into small tasks. If your goal is high, you probably will not be able to achieve it on your own. Disperse the powers and responsibilities to achieve the tasks.

6. Establish deadlines and send report cards. Everyone needs deadlines. To set priorities, you must set deadlines throughout the fundraising campaign.

7. Cultivate and update your lists of donors. Update your list of donors and submit it on a regular basis to your fundraising team. Also, from time to time, send it to all donors and potential donors.

8. Establish a challenge gift. Challenge donations are the most effective way to leverage donations.

9. Focus on Friend Raising. A successful recruitment campaign is a journey to develop close relationships with potential donors. The goal is to create a close and ongoing relationship between the donor and the organization. So, first focus on recruiting friends.

10. Just ask. The most important way to successfully fundraise is simply to ask. In his book *Mega Gifts*, Jerold Panas writes, "Many tenets are important, but the greatest of these is: You must ask for the gift. This may appear to be overly fundamental, but too often this cardinal principle is overlooked. The tongue gets heavy and thick, the hands perspire. But every salesperson knows that finally, inevitably - you must ask for the order. This is the greatest commandment of all."

# 4.

## DONATIONS FROM ABROAD

As was mentioned, the most important source of donations for NGOs is from abroad, and mainly from the United States. Israel is in ninth place among the countries that receive grants from foundations in the United States. It is hard to imagine the world of Israeli philanthropy without the ongoing and generous support of philanthropists from abroad, especially Jewish philanthropists. Israel is one of the world's largest importers of philanthropic funds.[14] Despite being a developed Western country, Israel is a target for philanthropic activity that goes beyond the usual patterns of cross-border philanthropy, which is mainly directed to developing countries and countries of the former Soviet Union. Although most of the resources provided to other Western countries are directed to international organizations operating in developing countries and to international assistance, most of the resources directed to Israel are for internal needs in the country.[15]

The amount of donations from abroad dropped from 67 percent in 2006 to 60 percent of the total donations to NGOs in Israel in 2011.[16,17] Despite this decline in donations from abroad, they still constitute a substantial part of the total donations of NGOs in Israel. This is why most of the non-profit organizations, public institutions and national institutions in Israel are significantly based on donations from abroad. The public institutions and the national institutions maintain offices and employ professional fundraisers abroad. These institutions and particularly large non-profit organizations run "Friends of" associations all over the world, where businessmen and large donors are located. The role of "Friends of" associations is to raise awareness and recruit donors for the entities that they are promoting.

The establishment of a "Friends of " association abroad for a non-profit organization in Israel requires a lot of effort and resources, as well as good relations abroad. This is why very few small and medium-sized organizations have such a "Friends of" association. However, without a serious and influential presence abroad, fundraising is extremely difficult. There are, of course, representative offices in Israel of philanthropic foundations from abroad that donate to various non-profit organizations. In addition, many non-profit organizations send representatives for occasional overseas fundraising campaigns, but a stable and permanent basis for large donations from abroad requires the establishment of a "Friends of" association. An exciting idea, a clear vision, high potential for making an impact, credible leadership and a clear plan for measuring and evaluating the organization's activities increase the chances of recruiting donations and supporters abroad. Like in the establishment of a board of directors of a non-profit organization in Israel, the establishment of a "Friends of" association abroad also requires an exciting and influential leader. A personal relationship with such a leader, who personally believes in the leadership and identifies with the goals and objectives of the non-profit organization, can certainly ensure the initial nucleus of the "Friends of" association. Cultivating connections with people who are wealthy and influential abroad requires time and ongoing effort, but it is essential for the establishment of a "Friends of" association. The greater the influence and status of the person who heads it, the easier it will be to attract business people and other influential people to the "Friends of" association. In many ways, the establishment of a "Friends of" association abroad is like a private company going public. Members of the "Friends of" association become full partners in determining the goals and objectives of the non-profit organization and sometimes even in managing it. Nevertheless, in order to create a true partnership, the non-profit organizations must also be careful in choosing the donors that are most suitable for them. As in any partnership, in philanthropic partnerships sometimes differences of opinions erupt between the donors and the non-profit organizations being donated to. In non-profit organizations where there is not a fully trusting relationship between donors and the management, these differences of opinion can be destructive. Intelligent donors understand that their involvement in the non-profit organization must be based on total mutual trust with the organization's leading staff — a trust that no agreement can create. Such donors provide space for a variety of opinions and do not impose their opinion on the organization. Only this way can they generate leadership and ideas that will advance the organization to make the positive change for which it was established. Creating mutual trust between the donors and members of the "Friends of" association and the non-profit organization requires a continuous and ongoing effort. And, of course, working with donors and supporters from abroad requires full transparency, professional reporting and control procedures.

About a year after the establishment of Ofanim, when its pilot project in the Merhavim Regional Council was crowned a success, we decided to open the Friends of Ofanim in the United States. My friends and I worked on preparing the material in English and adapting it to the American audience. We had to think about the non-profit organization's message, vision and guiding values. We defined — in clear-cut, measurable terms — the goals and objectives that we wanted to achieve. In 2005, I turned to a friend, who for many years served as the lawyer of my company in the United States, for help and advice. Attorney Henry Levi, a smart Jewish man and a leading business lawyer, immediately answered the challenge and began to examine and investigate the matter on a completely pro-bono basis. Henry, who until then had had little contact with Israel, surprised me with his immediate enlistment to the idea. He performed all of the registrations required by American law to set up the Friends of Ofanim association in the United States. He even succeeded in enlisting an accountant, and he got the new organization recognized by the IRS for donations (501c(3)) — on a completely volunteer basis. The amazing commitment of Henry and his friends led to the fact that in a very short period of time we succeeded in setting up Friends of Ofanim and gaining the important recognition for donations. After the establishment of the organization, Henry was pleased when I asked him to be a member of the board of Friends of Ofanim.

As a top-notch professional, Henry decided to visit Israel to closely observe the activities of the organization that he is representing. It was his first visit to Israel, and it had ignited an ancient spark in Henry that drew him even more into the matter. It seems that his connection to the children of Israel and his commitment to Ofanim, which was absolute even before the visit, had really turned into a mission. For many years Henry served as the secretary and lawyer of Friends of Ofanim, and he gave his professional services on an entirely volunteer basis. Although I worked with Henry for more than 15 years in business, the real and close friendship between us developed and deepened particularly during the years that we worked as volunteers for Ofanim. It appears that a volunteer basis, free of economic interests, is fertile ground for true friendships. In 2011, Henry died of a serious illness. In one of our last conversations, he pointed out that one of the most important and meaningful things he had done in his life was his involvement with the children of Ofanim. The fact that he saw fit to emphasize to me what he had done for the sake of the children of Israel warmed my heart, especially in light of the great achievements he had made in the professional field.

Working with members of Friends of Ofanim, like Henry, touched and excited me each time anew; the absolute commitment, the deep and true caring and the sincere concern each of these wonderful and special people have for the children of Israel is not to be taken for granted. Their genuine, pure and special giving to children they have never met is a living testimony to faith in the spirit of man, which was written about by the poet Shaul Tchernichovsky: "*For I still believe in man, in his spirit, his spirit of strength.*" After Henry's death, members of the board of Friends of Ofanim dedicated a laboratory in his memory, in cooperation with some of his many friends, and equipped it with the best technology for the well-being of the children of Ofanim. The establishment of Friends of Ofanim, which has become a full partner with Ofanim in Israel, will be forever accredited to Henry.

World Jewry is going through many changes, especially American Jewry. These changes reinforce the downward trend in donations to Israel. Commitment to the State of Israel among the younger generation of world Jewry is not as strong as that of their parents. The parents' generation, who personally experienced the Holocaust and witnessed the wonder of the establishment of the State of Israel, had a strong emotional bond with Israel. That generation saw it as a supreme duty to mobilize in droves to strengthen the young state that was a home for the survivors and refugees. Today, a large portion of the younger generation of world Jewry has been freed from these feelings and sees Israel as a strong and developed country, and is more suspicious and critical of it than its parents. For many, the aim of Tikkun Olam is no longer confined to Israel alone but to the entire world. Moreover, a large part of the younger generation's donations is directed at strengthening Jewish identity through local institutions and communities. In addition, the strengthening of the economy and the wealth that has accumulated in Israel in recent decades reduces the pressure on world Jewry to donate to Israel.

Years ago, a well-known Jewish American philanthropist who is a friend of mine, one of the first donors of Ofanim, told me that when he landed for the first time in the new airport in Israel — Ben Gurion 2000 — he immediately felt that "Israel had made a severe mistake." According to him, whenever he landed at the crumbling old airport, he "felt a strong need to take out his checkbook and write a check to donate to needy Israel." Now, with an airport that is newer, higher quality and more luxurious than many US airports, he feels that rich Israel is no longer in need of his donations.

The change in the patterns of world Jewry's giving is consistent with the recent changes in the patterns of global giving of established veteran immigrant communities. Donations from corporations, communities and individuals that in the past were directed to support programs and projects for a particular ethnic and national population, out of a sense of obligation to recognize its unmet needs, are now directed to more needy communities that do not necessarily belong to the same ethnic group. The guiding principle for global donors is the broad and universal view of the needs of populations in different locations and countries. Loyalty to the ethnic group is being replaced by addressing universal needs without ethnic, geographical or territorial affiliation.

Global philanthropy includes cross-border transfers of

funds, special grants, "in goods" and volunteers working to support and respond to the various needs outside their country. Philanthropy, money transfers and private capital investments are the three largest sources of cross-border transfers. In 2010, total worldwide transfers amounted to 575 billion dollars. This amount is four times greater than the Official Development Assistance, which totaled 128 billion dollars that year. Beyond that, universal philanthropy is looking for new and additional channels to donate to. The aim is to develop ideas, initiatives and programs that are innovative and breakthrough, of thinking outside the box.[18] As mentioned above, the younger generation of Diaspora Jewry is no different than the new global donors. Therefore, as the emotional connection of the younger generation of Diaspora Jewry to Israel loosens, and as the economic situation in Israel improves, the flow of donations from abroad will weaken.

# 5.

## INCOME FROM THE SALE OF SERVICES AND BUSINESS PHILANTHROPY

The growing competition over the limited sources of donations requires finding innovative financing methods and a range of income sources. Indeed, reality is not simple, but what can be done in such a situation? Quite a bit, as it turns out; one way to reduce dependence on classical philanthropy is to generate revenue by selling services. As a rule, there is no prohibition against generating profit in a non-profit organization — or in a public benefit corporation — but its main activity must be the promotion of non-business objectives. After years of ambiguity on the matter on the part of the Israeli government, in 2012 the Corporations Authority published the "Instructions of the Registrar of Non-profit Organizations regarding business activity by the non-profit organization." The legislator understood the difficulty and dependence of non-profit organizations on fundraising, and therefore published guidelines that allow business activity — within the non-profit organization or as a subsidiary of the non-profit organization — that can contribute to the advancement of the objectives while making optimal use of resources, and determined that this activity is permitted and even desirable, provided that it is carried out in accordance with the provisions of the law.[19]

Many non-profit organizations have developed unique knowledge and skills. On one hand, leveraging this knowledge and these skills can generate income that will enable economic independence, thereby reducing dependence on donations. But on the other hand, introducing a business aspect of providing services in a non-profit organization — or as a subsidiary of the non-profit organization — requires a different conduct mode than the non-profit organization was used to. The sale of services requires professionalism and standards used in the business world, mainly considerations of profit and loss.

The transition from a purely social model to a social model with business elements changes the non-profit organization's genetic code and the discourse within the non-profit organization. Therefore, despite the advantages and temptation to ease the pressure of the fundraising race, this transition must be discussed and planned with utmost caution and meticulousness. It appears that the growing need for resources and the huge competition for the limited pool of donations will necessarily lead more non-profit organizations in this direction. The key to success in this transition will be finding the right balance between keeping the genetic code of the non-profit organization and developing business capabilities. It is very important that this effort does not harm the focus on the main social objectives for which the organization was founded.

In addition to this trend, there has recently been an important development in the field of international philanthropy in general, and in Israel in particular, which is business philanthropy. This development blurs the boundaries between the business sector and the social sector. Social-for-profit enterprises are initiatives that combine social characteristics with a business model. In this model of a business-social combination, shareholders choose to conduct philanthropic activity that earmarks a large part of their profits to promote the social objective of the business.

In this matter too, there is development and recognition by the Israeli legislator, who understood the supreme importance of the third sector to society and made it possible to develop new tools that integrate social action with business activity. A "social business" is defined by the law as "business activity in a non-profit organization or in a public benefit corporation (PBC), which is directly related to the goals of the non-profit organization or the PBC, which (in the activity) itself actualizes social goals. In this business activity, the corporation strives to profit, but not to maximize its profits as a result of its social objectives," or "a company whose activity is aimed at fulfilling social objectives, and that it (in the activity) in itself is intended to achieve the fulfillment of the social objectives determined in its statute, which seeks to profit but not to maximize its profits as a result of its social objectives, and whose articles stipulate a limit on the withdrawal of profits by private investors, if any, in the company, that will not exceed 50 percent of the distributable profits. This restriction will apply only after the withdrawal of profits in the amount of the equity investments of the company's shareholders"[20]

In most of the world's developed countries, donations are made through philanthropic foundations. In Israel, the "third addendum" to the Israeli Companies Law, which regulates the establishment of investment funds for public benefit, was added in 2014.[21] This addendum opens up possibilities for raising capital from the public for social businesses. Like in the business capital market, in which companies raise capital from the public in order to develop their businesses in return for shares or bonds, a social capital market will enable social businesses to raise capital from the public in return for partial ownership of the social-business initiative and potential for partial repayment of its investment. Investment in a social-business initiative will also enable the social investor to influence the objectives and conduct of the initiative. The advantage of these initiatives is the adoption of codes of effective business conduct for managing the initiative. In addition, instead of maximizing economic profit, the initiative tries to balance social goals with the basic needs that enable its financial sustainability. In early 2015, the state launched a tender for the establishment of two public benefit funds. It was won by the IVN and the Dualis Social Investment Fund. The state, for its part, allocated 20 million NIS, and in return, the foundations committed to transferring 50 million NIS to social businesses for three years from the date of its establishment.

It is too early to see how this amendment to the law will affect the amount of money that will be allocated to the social sector. Will the general public, investment funds and corporations respond to this new challenge? Will this amendment lead to the redirection of new money to the third sector or the channeling of funds earmarked for donations to these social businesses? There is no doubt that social businesses are not suitable for all of the types of social activity. There are many special populations and needs that must be answered on a purely philanthropic basis. Non-profit organizations that provide responses to these special needs will always have to rely on donations and support.

The ultimate financial anchor for a non-profit organization is an endowment fund for the non-profit organization's objectives. These funds are more popular in the United States. The main idea of these funds is to ensure the financial sustainability of the non-profit organization over time by ensuring a steady income for the non-profit organization from the fund's profits. Donors who the non-profit organization is important to them and who wish to ensure its existence over the years collect enough money so that the annual interest of the fund — the profit — is transferred each year as a donation to the non-profit organization's operation. But endowment funds require huge sums and tremendous commitment from donors. For example, an organization with a budget of 3 million dollars will have to set up a fund of 100 million dollars, assuming that the annual interest rate that the fund can attain is three percent. But an organization with an endowment fund will no longer need to worry about fundraising, unless it decides to expand its activities beyond the annual income from the endowment fund. Raising such huge sums for a fund is not easy; one of the common techniques for raising such high amounts is through the donation of life insurance. In such cases, the non-profit organization's donors are asked to buy a life insurance policy and register the endowment fund as the policy beneficiary in case of death. The donor actually pays the annual premium, and only in the event of death does the high amount of the insurance go to the endowment fund.

Establishing an endowment fund is not a trivial act. It requires very committed donors to the organization and ongoing efforts to recruit such donors. This is the reason why only a few organizations manage to establish endowment funds. There are donors who on principle are unwilling to donate to endowment funds because they believe that non-profit organizations which do not have to make an effort to fundraise are in danger of moral corruption and stagnation. On the other hand, there are donors who see the non-profit organization's economic sustainability over time as an opportunity for the non-profit organization to deal with the most important core issues and not with Sisyphean fundraising efforts. In any event, non-profit organizations that are able to set up an endowment fund and collect the huge sums that are needed are non-profit organizations that have reached a state of tranquility.

It is important to remember that one of the problems of philanthropy in Israel is the multiple duplications of non-profit organizations. Many non-profit organizations operate in overlapping areas for the achievement of similar objectives and even in identical target audiences. Connections, collaborations and mergers of many non-profit organizations may lead to cooperation, effectiveness, enormous savings and strengthening of the non-profit organizations. The desire to leave a mark and often also egoistic considerations have led to a situation in which there are almost no mergers between non-profit organizations in Israel. In this sense, it is important to remember the statement of the ninth president of the State of Israel, Shimon Peres: "Each person is as small as his ego, and as great as the subject he serves." The great fragmentation of the Israeli non-profit sector is a sign of its non-ripeness and immaturity. As the social sector develops — and matures — more mergers amongst non-profit organizations will take place. The ongoing competition over the pool of limited resources and the rise in the establishment of social-business initiatives have the potential to change and encourage mergers amongst non-profit organizations.

# CHAPTER SEVEN:

# CHECKING OURSELVES

*With a proper measuring stick it is possible to manage any organization.*

- Lee Iacocca

# 1.

## EVALUATION AND MEASUREMENT

Social action is not measured only by its direct output, as venture capital investment is not only measured by the return on investment, rather also by the enormous impact on the economy in general and on technological developments in particular. As in the business sector, also in the social sector, the effectiveness of an organization is measured in relation to return on investment (ROI). In the business world, return is mainly measured in financial profitability, whereas yields in the social world are the level of ability and effectiveness in fulfilling the organization's mission. Social action has byproducts and makes broad impacts on Israeli society in general. The very act of social involvement is an important and valuable statement of mutual responsibility, solidarity and social resilience. However, as was mentioned, each organization must strive for continuous improvement and measure its effectiveness in a reliable, professional and continuous manner. Despite the lack of agreement on methods and measurement standards for measuring the effectiveness of non-profit organizations, it is of utmost importance to carry out a process of evaluation and measurement in non-profit organizations, even more so than in the business world. Every social organization, whatever its purpose may be, can and must measure the level of its performance by determining key performance indicators that are appropriate through a combination of quantitative and qualitative measures. A non-profit organization that does not measure its effectiveness in a professional and reliable manner is betraying the trust of its donors and the supporters of its activities. The evaluation and measurement process must be part of the organization's culture and practice and not just a marginal process intended only for having something to present to potential donors.

The enormous competition for resources and the growing professionalism of the third sector in Israel make evaluation and measurement a vital and existential matter. Effectiveness is the main criterion in the considerations of new donors and social investors. These donors and social investors, who come from a business background, demand rigid measurement outputs for their social investment. In order for an organization to fulfill its mission in the most effective way, its decision-making process must be professional and based on valid, reliable and significant data. The evaluation and measurement process should provide data and information in a reliable and accurate manner, enabling the organization's leaders to make informed decisions, to choose effective courses of action and to reach correct operational conclusions.

The main purpose of evaluation and measurement is to help the organization examine its performance in relation to its defined goals and objectives so that it can make adjustments when actual performance deviates from the plans. A reliable and professional evaluation and measurement process supports better management of programs and organizations. But despite the utmost importance, the challenge of evaluation and measurement in the third sector is far from simple or from being understood. In Israel, little use is made of evaluation and measurement. Some of the non-profit organizations do not have a full understanding of the process and its importance to the organization and usually view it as a marginal thing. Many organizations give it to outside experts to perform. They see it as cumbersome and irrelevant work, carried out for the purposes of reporting and accountability. Contrary to statements by some social leaders regarding the importance of the evaluation and measurement process, it appears that its inherent potential as far as planning, improvement, learning and decision making has not been realized.[1] It could be said that many people talk about evaluation and measurement, but few truly evaluate and measure.

A few years ago, I attended a conference of heads of philanthropic foundations that took place in the United States, in which the main theme was evaluation and measurement. The keynote speakers at the conference were two prominent businessmen and big Jewish philanthropists, both major and central supporters of two important non-profit organizations in Israel. The main theme throughout the conference, which was concluded by two main lectures given by these knowledgeable people, was, "We measure everything we do — in business and in philanthropy." This clear message, which came from highly successful businessmen, each in his own field, sounded very reliable and left its mark on the conference participants. Yet, I left there frustrated and confused, because I was very familiar with the non-profit organizations they talked about, and I knew first-hand about their directors' ongoing frustration with their inability to measure and evaluate their activities. These non-profit organizations do holy work and provide very vital activities, but on the topic of evaluation and measurement, I understood that there was a serious gap between statements and actions. Unfortunately, this gap and the confusion regarding evaluation and measurement are something that many non-profit organizations in Israel face. Important efforts are being made in this area all over the world, which are yielding significant progress and proper attention. To date, however, there is no correct answer, perfect approach or even set of approaches that will solve the needs of the social sector. Also, the fact that the activities of many non-profit organizations are comprised of long-term processes that seek to make qualitative changes, such as changes in attitude or behavior, adds to the complexity and difficulty in evaluation and measurement. The lack of clarity regarding measurement objectives often creates confusion and a mismatch of expectations. This confusion stems, among other things, from a lack of agreement and acceptance of classification terms for assessing and measuring non-profit organizations' performance. This lack of agreement and the fact that almost every non-profit organization in Israel has its own unique "measuring stick," blemishes the reliability of the measurement and makes it difficult to create an effective comparison of the various organizations. There is ambiguity and inconsistency in the measurement language and measurement terms. People often use synonyms in the terms, such as "results," "effectiveness" and "impact," without having a common or precise understanding of those terms. It is no wonder, then, that there are people who doubt the processes of evaluation and measurement. Some of them were disappointed by the process results that did not justify the many resources that were invested in them. Some rely on intuition in making good decisions, which makes them continue to behave according to their gut feelings. One of the main causes of disappointment in evaluation and measurement processes stems from the lack of direction of the process for practical measurement and the integration of its results in the organization's decision-making process, as well as a lack of understanding of the objectives of the process. The evaluation and measurement process can have various aspects, such as accountability, creation of knowledge and academic value. In general, the goals of the process can be divided into three simple and distinct categories:

1. Reporting what was done with the allocated resources.
2. Collecting information that can assist in making decisions.
3. A systematic study of proven practical methods for solving certain social problems.[2,3]

Despite the difficulties and lack of agreement on measurement, every social organization, whatever its purpose may be, can and must measure itself through a combination of quantitative and qualitative measures. Each organization can and must determine its own key performance indicators by which it examines its performance in relation to the main objectives that it has set for itself. These indicators help the organization quantify its progress towards achieving its goals. A social organization that does not measure itself in a reliable and professional manner is not worthy of the trust and support of its donors and supporters. An organization that does not implement an evaluation and measurement process is an organization that cannot be managed because "you cannot manage what you don't measure."

Since evaluation and measurement have become part of the mainstream discourse in the third sector and often also a basic donor demand, pressure has been put on non-profit organizations to present measurement reports of their activities' outcomes. This pressure often leads to the perspective that the evaluation and measurement process is something incidental and external, that is done for the sake of presenting it to donors, social investors and groups outside of the organization, rather than as something that is useful and essential to the organization's decision-making process. To fulfill this obligation, these non-profit organizations focus on measuring values that are simple, easy and available, yet do not necessarily indicate the effectiveness of their activities. Moreover, there are organizations that exploit the lack of understanding of evaluation and measurement held by some of the donors and attribute themselves to achievements that have nothing to do with them.

Years ago, a potential donor asked me about the measuring methods of Ofanim. I explained to him at length about the methodology and the indices used in the organization's areas of activity. These are measures that consist of a combination of qualitative and quantitative parameters according to accepted standards in this field. I then sensed that the potential donor — who came from the business sector and had no knowledge of the field of education — was having difficulty understanding or accepting the qualitative measurements. He claimed that he was donating to a similar non-profit organization in one of Israel's major cities, where they measure only quantitatively. I told him it sounds very interesting, and I would be happy to learn what and how they measure so that we can adopt their methods in Ofanim. The truth is that I was very surprised because I was familiar with that non-profit organization, and I knew that it was not possible to measure its activity only by quantitative measures.

A few weeks later, he forwarded me an email that he received from the CEO of the non-profit organization regarding their quantitative measures. I was surprised to find at the top of the list of indicators the impressive percentage increase in the number of students in the city — without any connection to the non-profit organization — who completed high school with full matriculation in the year in which the organization began to operate, compared to years after it started to operate. I couldn't understand how an organization could take the credit for the increase in the number of students in the city who finish high school with a matriculation certificate, without any connection to the organization's direct contribution to the matter, while completely ignoring the contribution of the formal education system, and the many NGOs and organizations operating in that city in those areas. The strong desire to boast about achievements in order to win the attention of potential donors is quite a temptation for non-profit organizations. A small number of them have fallen into this temptation, causing damage to the rest of the non-profit organizations and the third sector in general.

It is not only the non-profit organizations that have confusion regarding the evaluation and measurement of non-profit organizations, but also the donors and the supporters. Many donors do not understand the complexities and nuances of measurement processes in different fields. Many of the non-profit organizations seek to make social changes that require time and standards that are different than those in the business world. But non-profit organizations must remain loyal to themselves and an absolute commitment to ethical, honest, reliable and professional conduct. A deep understanding of the importance of a reliable, professional and uncompromising measurement process will ultimately bring both the appropriate donors and their appreciation.

The difficulty in measuring the effectiveness of non-profit organizations led to the establishment of various groups to evaluate and rank the effectiveness of social organizations and non-profit organizations according to various criteria (for example, Raising for Effective Giving, GiveWell). Also in Israel, several infrastructure organizations have been established to supervise, rank and assist non-profit organizations, such as Midot, whose goal is to promote effectiveness as a key criterion in the consideration of social investors and in the management of non-profit organizations.

This is through rating of non-profit organizations and the implementation of field reports and activities to change the public discourse. Midot assesses non-profit organizations chances of being effective. Meaning, to create social value and to bring about a change for the better in the lives of their beneficiaries, and issues a "Seal of Effectiveness" accordingly.[4]

Another important group is the organization Sheatufim, which specializes in managing complex partnership and discourse processes in order to promote social impact. Underlying the Sheatufim activity is the understanding that in order to create a significant change in society, it is necessary to utilize the three sectors — the public (government), the business and the social sectors — for a common goal and in providing professional tools for managing the process. GuideStar, a non-profit initiative that was established within and for civil society, in cooperation with the Ministry of Justice, collects and presents regulatory information originating from governmental authorities and information from the organizations themselves, about NGOs, without taking any position or passing judgment. These infrastructure organizations and others do great work and add to the professionalism of the social sector. However, regarding the effectiveness rating of non-profit organizations, there is still no single authority that does this that is accepted by everyone. The absence of a common language of measurement and the lack of agreement over accepted indicators for the evaluation and measurement of non-profit organizations' activity has created opposition among non-profit organizations to there being an external body that would measure and rate them according to their effectiveness. It created even more vehement opposition among the young non-profit organizations, who are concerned about being harmed by such a rating because they do not have a long history of activity. In addition, an infrastructure organization can conduct audits on the financial resilience, the institutional integrity, the level of management involvement, etc., but not on the measure of the effectiveness of an organization's core activity. This process requires domain knowledge of the non-profit organization's area of activity, and also requires time, energy and resources to have an in-depth understanding of the operational methodology, the target audience, the unique problems, the possible solutions and the impact of the non-profit organization over time.

A serious, reliable and professional evaluation and measurement process must be carried out by the non-profit organization itself, sometimes with the participation of experts and external professional bodies. Donors and social investors must demand this from the non-profit organizations that they finance. This requires greater knowledge and involvement of donors and supporters in determining the indices and methods of measurement. It is important to remember that evaluation and measurement is not an exogenous process — separate and external — to the organization. It should be ingrained in the culture and practice of the organization. However, there are several cultural factors that prevent Israeli non-profit organizations from adopting evaluative thinking and integrating it into the practice and culture of their organization:

1. **Few decisions are made on a factual basis.** Measurement and evaluation improve organizational activity by distinguishing between proven and successful practices and other methods that do not produce the desired results.

2. **Fear that evaluation and measurement will suppress emotion, passion and compassion.** Measurement and evaluation should not come at the expense of passion and emotion. On the contrary, the knowledge that what we are doing is working and the ability to improve and be improved should feed this passion.

3. **Skepticism about even the possibility of measuring social programs.** This skepticism stems mainly from a lack of understanding that it is possible to scientifically and professionally measure the activities of non-profit organizations that operate for qualitative changes.

4. **Costs, time and high inputs.** Evaluation and measurement processes are long processes that require a lot of energy and resources from the professional staff, which deters many from conducting them.

5. **Lack of priorities leads to focusing on burning issues at the expense of strategy and infrastructure.** The human resources of many non-profit organizations, especially the younger ones, are very limited and overloaded. The many tasks required in implementing the non-profit organization's activities do not leave them the time or availability to deal

with processes that require time, resources and energy.

6. **Lack of recognition of the advantages of the evaluation and measurement process.** Many non-profit organizations see the evaluation and measurement process as something separate and external to the organization's activities. A professional evaluation and measurement process that is carried out in an open manner in the organization brings all involved parties, especially the donors, supporters, board of directors and the management team, to a clear and common understanding of the objectives for which they operate. The process reflects, sharpens and validates the basic assumptions on which the organization is founded. It instills a new spirit of vitality and gives professional validation to activity, and mainly gets all those involved focused in the most efficient way on achieving the objective for which it was established.

7. **The passion that brings people into the third sector makes some of them act intuitively and emotionally, instead of in a rational manner based on facts.** I often hear people in social action say, "We do not have to evaluate and measure, we know that what we are doing is working." The evaluation and measurement process has many advantages beyond measuring whether things "work."[6] About five years after the founding of Ofanim, I renewed my connection with a dear and beloved childhood friend. This friend had taken a track in life that was very similar and parallel to mine. He grew up with me in the same

neighborhood, we played the same games with the same friends. We studied in the same school and were in the same class, and to this day his parents live within touching distance of my parents' house. In our first meeting after many years, we had a long conversation and we filled in the gaps. Toward the end of the meeting, I told him that I wanted to present to him something I had been working on in recent years. I gave him a short presentation on Ofanim. Until that moment, he had heard absolutely nothing about the organization. At the end of the presentation, there was silence in the room, and his eyes suddenly filled up with tears. I saw in his eyes the tremendous understanding of the need for Ofanim, an understanding that comes from our shared experience in the difficult environment in which we grew up. After a few moments, he said, "It's such a shame that during our childhood we didn't have an Ofanim lab like this — it could have saved a lot of our friends." I didn't have to explain to him the significance and tremendous value I saw in the non-profit organization's activities.

He later joined the board of directors of Ofanim, and despite the deep understanding of the tremendous need and of the potential impact of the organization's activities, we have become among the most urging and supportive people of the process for evaluation and measurement of Ofanim. In other words, a process of evaluation and measurement does not "replace" the deep feelings of the need and vitality of the organization's activity, but rather it confirms, reinforces, complements, strengthens and intensifies them.

# 2.

## CONSTANT STRIVING FOR IMPROVEMENT

Every organization should constantly strive to improve, but in order to improve, one must first know what needs improvement. Therefore, non-profit organizations must implement, as an integral part of their activities, evaluation and measurement processes, based on the systematic use of data. The board of directors should outline specific and clear measures for the organization's managers since these operate according to the manner in which they are measured. In order to make logical decisions, it is essential to set appropriate and detailed "key performance indicators." Defining clear objectives of the process and detailed strategies for achieving them are essential to the success of the process. The objectives describe what success will look like, and the strategies outline the ways of achieving it. A proper mix of stable management, strict conduct and constant dedication to achieving results enables the organization to fulfill its mission. Although strategic planning is not a luxury, the planning process demands significant investment of resources, as well as organizational courage. Non-profit organizations must invest resources to plan and collect and analyze information, acquire and adapt technologies and measurement tools and often employ external evaluation and measurement consultants. Many organizations are unable to invest the inputs and resources necessary for the success of the process, so they have difficulty measuring their output. This is particularly true for young non-profit organizations that are struggling for the meager resources that are at their disposal.

Donors and supporters must understand that planning and implementing strategies and evaluation and measurement methods require allocation of inputs, funding, time and energy beyond the direct costs of operating the programs themselves. Therefore, they must see the costs of the evaluation and measurement process as an integral part of the program costs they finance rather than as overhead or indirect expenses. Donors and supporters should not aim to minimize spending, but rather to maximize impact. And to maximize impact, organizations need time and adequate overhead support. Donors and program sponsors can be significantly involved in evaluating programs. There are several other stakeholders in the evaluation and measurement process, and often with conflicting interests. The participation of all stakeholders in the evaluation and measurement process improves the quality of the process, increases the chances of its success and creates an open and productive atmosphere.[7,8]

The process of evaluation and measurement is gradual, takes a long time and requires ripeness and maturity of everyone involved. Evaluation and measurement cannot be transformed into an integral part of the organization's activity with one quick decision. An organization that does not evaluate and measure its activities cannot suddenly decide to commission external evaluation experts to carry out an evaluation and measurement process for it. A real process is introspection and intense consideration, first of all, of the organization internally. It is desirable and necessary to involve evaluation and measurement consultants in the internal process in order to create a proper and professional infrastructure for continuous and consistent evaluation and measurement. The process requires preparation, internalization and deep involvement of all concerned within the organization. But it is important to remember that there are ups and downs in the process; it requires patience and consistency. The internal process creates a common language, and the concepts, assumptions, goals and practical steps to achieving them gradually become sharper and clearer. An external process must come as a complementary and validating step to this process.

For an organization to perform or to order a professional evaluation and measurement, a basic familiarity with, and even mastery of, the various skills and methods of evaluation and measurement is required. After selecting the appropriate methods for the organization, they should be implemented and integrated into all areas of the organization's activity in a continuous manner and not only in a separate program. Organizations that are proficient in relevant measurement methods know which key indicators are to be examined, what the important data is, how to collect it and how to translate it into knowledge and utilize it to improve their activities. These skills are the first vital step that organizations that want to fulfill their mission must take. Non-profit organizations that carry out a strategic planning process to examine their activities and identify indicators for monitoring their progress stand out as having a good sense of direction, and from time to time apply measurement tools to check whether they are on track to achieving their objectives.

Beyond the products that the evaluation and measurement processes produce for the managers of the non-profit organizations, they are also an investment prerequisite for many donors and social investors. Therefore, in order to validate the findings, it is very important that the professional group that participates in the implementation of the independent evaluation and measurement be recognized, has authority, and a reputation in the field. Sometimes donors and social investors from the business sector — where evaluation and measurement are mostly quantitative — erroneously think that non-profit organizations must also measure only quantitatively. Many organizations operate in long-term processes to change habits, attitudes or trends that are not quantifiable in quantitative ways only. Today, evaluation data can be collected using qualitative methods such as observations, interviews, etc., and quantitative methods such as surveys, statistical analyses of actual evaluations that were made, etc. Despite the many disagreements about the best strategies and data types, today it seems that both quantitative and qualitative measurements are valuable and can both be carefully analyzed.[9]

In general, a measurement process consists of four basic steps (see Chart number 9). The first stage is to define the objectives of the non-profit organization in "practical" terms called concept operationalization. Many non-profit organizations set an objective of making long-term social changes. Such objectives are usually defined in abstract terms, such as non-profit organizations for closing social gaps, for changing the culture of giving in society, for increasing social solidarity, for changing patterns of behavior in society and so on. These behavioral concepts represent complexities of activities, intentions, feelings and phenomena that are difficult to directly predict. It is sometimes difficult to estimate these abstract concepts in the evaluation and measurement process because measuring change of attitudes or behavior does not have objective results such as measuring height, length or weight, which can be directly measured. The challenge of direct quantitative measurement is finding a reliable and accepted measuring instrument. But when trying to measure abstract concepts, such as empowerment, there must be a fundamental and complete understanding of the concept, the definition of the concepts in a more practical manner, before you can have a general idea of the appropriate "key performance indicators" and the type of measurements that can be used for them. An abstract concept must be clearly labeled and defined. The labeling and definition of the abstract concept make it possible to relate, identify and communicate it as something known and familiar. The prominent characteristics, the traits and the precise criteria of the concept are the components that differentiate between one abstract concept and another.[10] A clearer and more "useful" definition of these abstract concepts makes the hypotheses underlying them operative. To underscore the difficulty of this process, some researchers compare it to building a rope bridge across a chasm between the world of ideas and the world of observations.[11] For example, the declared mission of Ofanim is to "bring educational wealth and empowerment to children in the remote locations of Israel in order to encourage their aspirations for higher education and to contribute to themselves and to society at large." The rationale of Ofanim is to create positive and empowering "key experiences" for the children of the small and remote locations, similar to the key experience I had with Prof. Bergman, and the release of inner energy in these children, which will bring a large portion of them to actualize their full potential. After endless discussions amongst the boards of Friends of Ofanim, Ofanim, and in professional committees with top experts in the field of informal education in Israel, we translated the meta-goal of the Ofanim into several achievable goals, each of which can be measured:

1. To reach as many children as possible in the small and remote communities and expose them to the sciences, technology and math (STEM) through mobile laboratories and other ways.
2. To hold enrichment and exposure activities in special programs, from new worlds of content, by a skilled and committed professional team.
3. To strengthen children's sense of ability and self-efficacy, to develop thinking, expression and communication skills, and to stimulate curiosity.

4. To strengthen the participants' motivation to learn and succeed, and to get closer to the world of higher education.

These goals were chosen because many studies in the field have shown that children who are curious, who have a sense of high self-efficacy and those with a recognition and understanding of the importance of higher education for success in life are more likely to reach academia than children without these characteristics. We then established the relevant key performance indicators and built an infrastructure for evaluating and measuring each of the practical objectives mentioned above. Special questionnaires were compiled, and interviews were conducted with children, parents, teachers and others at the beginning, middle and end of the year. This data was collected in a customized data system that was created for Ofanim for this purpose. The professional committee of Ofanim, which is comprised of researchers and experts in the field of measurement and evaluation, continuously examines, improves and enhances the organization's infrastructure and evaluation and measurement processes. Thus, these achievable goals were translated into measurable objectives:

Short-term objectives: Grades 3-6 - Enhancing self-efficacy, instilling learning and thinking skills, expression and communication skills, instilling knowledge in STEM and exposure to the academic world.

Medium-term objectives: Grades 7-9 – High level placement in STEM groups and eligibility for high matriculation diplomas.

Long-term objectives – Academic education.

The process of evaluation and measurement in Ofanim became an integral part of the non-profit organization's culture. These are continuous, ongoing and professional evaluation and measurement processes that are interwoven with the organization's activities. This was achieved thanks to the advice, direction and guidance from our Friends of Ofanim board members. On Friends of Ofanim's and Ofanim's board of directors are experts in educational evaluation and measurement processes, and on the professional committee are experts from the field of education. The internal processes measure the effectiveness of logistics, operations, drivers, counselors, coordinators, regional (north and south) operations managers, fundraising, the CEO, etc. Each counselor is required to fill in feedback at the end of each day of activity.

External processes measure the impact of the activity on students, parents, schools and the environment. Every few years the organization conducts external surveys by professional teams to validate and verify the results of internal evaluation and measurement processes. In a study conducted in 2016, when the graduates of the first years of operation of Ofanim completed high school, we conducted a large survey of graduates to examine the situation of the children of Ofanim. The survey was conducted by external researchers from the Technion and Tel-Hai College. The survey examined 119 graduates of Ofanim from its early years. The parents of 60 percent of these graduates do not have an academic education. The survey found that 23.5 percent of Ofanim graduates study in the five-unit track in mathematics, compared with the national average in the northern region of 8.2 percent and in the southern region of 6.9 percent.

56 percent of the survey participants study in between four and five units in mathematics, and 89 percent of them study in between four and seven units in English. In addition, 59 percent of them study in enhanced learning in at least one of the scientific or technological fields. The survey also found that 58 percent of Ofanim graduates expressed their intention and desire to continue their academic studies in the sciences (STEM). The survey participants expressed high satisfaction with Ofanim activities (4.37 out of five) and experienced the activities as pleasant and positive. These achievements especially stand out in light of the fact that most of the activities of Ofanim are concentrated in the small, remote and weak socio-economic peripheral communities.

The next step, after defining the goal in executable terms, is the definition of the measurement design. Research in the social sciences provides us with several approaches to achieving valid, reliable and useful measurements. These approaches help us define which data we need to collect, and the ways to collect it. None of these approaches can be considered better or preferable because the choice of one over the other depends on the context, the desired results to be measured, and the budget and time that is available.

The third stage is data collection. In this stage, measurement errors must be watched out for. But as in real life, here too not every process can be free of errors. Therefore, attention must be paid to two important sub-processes: error control and error measurement. These sub-processes are very important because errors can be reduced but cannot be avoided. In addition, we must know that errors always influence any estimates, and therefore knowing their magnitude can help improve the interpretation of measurement results.

Since raw data, for the most part, is not final information that can be used, a fourth step is needed — analysis, consideration and deep contemplation of data to provide insight for policy or decision making — data analysis. Data is a raw material that produces and provides information in various forms: from creating simple indicators — calculating the ratio between two measurements — to complex statistical analyses.

## The four basic stages of the measurement process

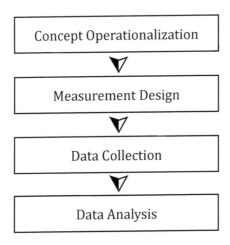

*Source: "Measurement and Effectiveness: Methodologies, Considerations, Issues and Possible Solutions, Stefano Campostrini, Chapter 18. 2005*

The ultimate aspiration of every non-profit organization must conclude that one day it and its activities will be completely unnecessary. In the dynamic world in which we live, many and frequent changes in the circumstances and reality in which non-profit organizations operate can significantly influence the necessity of their activities. To this end, non-profit organizations must examine themselves, their goals, processes and the underlying assumptions on which they are based. A real, reliable, professional and bold evaluation and measurement process enables us to examine changes in the field and to confirm or disprove the basic assumptions, as well as to make adjustments to the activities of the non-profit organization.

Rarely do changes in the field, circumstances and bureaucracy completely make the activity of one non-profit organization or another redundant. Seemingly, such a result is supposed to be a joyous event and a cause for celebration for every non-profit organization, but in my many years of social involvement I have not yet seen or heard of any non-profit organization announcing the end of its activities due to such happy circumstances. Sometimes it seems that the dependency of people on the non-profit organization and its transformation into an essential part of the identity and routine of the people involved in it, in fact, prevents them from recognizing the changing reality. In such a situation, instead of celebrating the conclusion of their role, the non-profit organizations continue to operate without a defined goal as "zombie organizations" — as a solution that seeks a problem. Such non-profit organizations are sinning against themselves, causing damage to the purpose for which they were established, and especially creating a bad reputation for the entire social sector. The existence of a reliable and professional evaluation and measurement process is a guarantee for preventing such sad situations.

In spite of all this, we certainly could say that in recent years the understanding of the importance of evaluation and measurement in the social sector in Israel has been growing. In addition, the new generation of donors, both from Israel and abroad, is a generation that strongly leans towards measurement, and the demand for evaluation and measurement processes as a prerequisite for contributions is increasing. Evaluation and measurement processes in non-profit organizations must be perceived as no less than part of the proper management of the non-profit organization. Only in this way can we learn, improve and generate the desired positive social change.

# CONCLUSION

*And who am I in this whole sequence*
*After all, life is not bought with money*
*It's bought with grace*
*And small deeds*

- Ishay Ribo

The social polarization, the lack of tolerance, the moral decline and the enormous social gaps constitute a real danger to the integrity of the Israeli society. Even though the state bears the ultimate responsibility for the gaps and the inequality levels, for anyone who deeply cares about Israel's values, resilience and moral image, indifference, apathy and lack of action are not really an option, because they constitute an unspoken agreement and a shared responsibility for perpetuating these gaps, which endanger our very existence here.

It's true, on one hand, the deep rifts can be paralyzing and cause despair, but on the other hand, they can also pose a great opportunity for us to shape the character of society and redefine the relationships among us. Social involvement and action have the power to create an understanding and a basis for dialogue and to lead to narrowing the social gaps and bridging the social rifts. Additionally, "The best in man," claims Albert Einstein, "can flourish only when he is involved and has immersed himself in a community."[1] Through joint social action, we expose our human sides and express solidarity and compassion toward the other and the different. This solidarity does not mean giving up on our opinions or disagreement on matters that are important to us, since in our tradition, as long as the disagreements are to the point of the matter, then they are the way to clarifying the truth. Also, social action and involvement make us more tolerant and allow us to work together to promote common objectives and issues despite the disagreements. They generate opportunities for us to get to know the other and the different as a whole, rather than through a narrow prism of labels and stereotypes.

Through social action, involvement and giving we have the ability to transform the society in which we live to an exemplary society— one that's ethical, sensitive, connected, considerate, caring and compassionate. In a communal society with a high level of social involvement, solidarity, respect and mutual responsibility prevail. This kind of communal society has the power to take the unproportionable power away from lobby groups, to expect and demand of its leaders ethical and moral behavior, to insist on more just and equal national-societal priorities. It is possible, and it depends only on us, on each one of us. Each person according to his abilities and in his own unique way can enrich the colorful rainbow of the communal-social action in Israel with his own unique shade. According to Rabbi Soloveitchik, the individuals who belong to such a communal society "complement one another." He added, "Each individual possesses something unique, rare, which is unknown to others; each individual has a unique message to communicate, a special color to add to the communal spectrum. Hence, when an individual joins the community, he adds a new dimension to the community awareness. He contributes something that no one else could have contributed. He enriches the community existentially; he is irreplaceable."[2]

Throughout life, we meet good people who, through their actions, add a special color to our lives. One of these good people is Israel Cohen, who was one of the principals at the boarding school where I studied in Kfar Maimon. During my studies, I suffered from gum problems in my mouth. When I could no longer bear the pain, I went to see a dentist in Be'er Sheva to check the problem. The dentist who treated me determined that I had to undergo a procedure that would cost 1,200 shekels, an amount that was beyond my financial capabilities. When I returned to Kfar Maimon, I bumped into Israel Cohen who asked me from where I was coming. I told him about the examination and its outcome, and I told him that I would apparently have to just live with the problem since I didn't have any way to pay for the treatment. A few days later, Israel called me over to him and he handed me an envelope. I opened it and found a personal check in his name for the amount of 1,200 shekels. "Take it, you don't have to live with the problem, go have the procedure done," he said. I was very moved by the gesture and did not stop thanking him. I knew even then that Israel Cohen was not a well-to-do man and that paying for the procedure was not simple for him either. I felt that I owed him a huge debt, but at least I would have to pay him back the money. Therefore, I decided that on Fridays — a day in which the children of the boarding school, most of whom lived in nearby communities, would go home for a visit and return before the start of Shabbat — I would do private landscaping work at different houses in Kfar Maimon in order to make some money and save up the amount to repay my debt.

Decades later, I visited one of the first activities of Ofanim in Tushia Village, which is adjacent to Kfar Maimon where I had studied. When I arrived, a woman approached me, introduced herself and said, "Well done. You guys are really doing holy work, I don't know how to thank you all. My daughter eagerly awaits the arrival of the Ofanim mobile lab." Suddenly she disappeared and after a few minutes, she returned with a tray of Moroccan donuts. "You have to taste this, I made it especially for you all." The woman went out of her way to shower the organization with compliments and didn't stop praising the counselors, the activities and the importance of it all to the children. After she calmed down, I told her that I was a graduate of the boarding school in the nearby Kfar Maimon Village and I asked her if she knew Israel Cohen who was the principal of the boarding school. "Yes, of course I know him," she answered, "unfortunately he passed away about two years ago. But do you see that girl over there, the one sitting next to my daughter?" She pointed to one of the girls who was participating in Ofanim's mobile laboratory activity, "That's Tal, Israel's granddaughter. She is my daughter's best friend." My heart skipped a beat and my eyes filled with tears.

About eight years after that encounter in Tushia Village, during a visit of US Friends of Ofanim's members in Israel, I accompanied them to see Ofanim's activity in Shokeda Village, near Tushia. The management presented two twelfth grade girls, graduates of the organization's activities. They spoke about the implications that the experience had on them. The graduates told about how the Ofanim's activities had been very meaningful and empowering for them, exposing them to sciences, which caused them to choose to study in science tracks in high school. They also added that they were both intending to continue their studies for bachelor's degrees in science. After the meeting, I approached one of the graduates and asked her if she happened to know Tal, Israel's granddaughter. "Of course," she answered, "she is a good friend of mine and she also participated in Ofanim's activities." I asked her for Tal's telephone number. A few days later, I called Tal, introduced myself, and I asked her if she remembered the Ofanim activities and how it affected her. Her response was as enthusiastic as that of her friends. I told her about my acquaintance with her grandfather and the act of kindness he had done for me when I was a child. "You're making me cry," she excitedly admitted. I told her that her grandfather's good deed would accompany me my entire life, and I felt that a little circle of grace had been closed. I understood then the deeper meaning of the verse from Ecclesiastes: "Send your bread forth upon the waters;

for after many days you will find it."

And how can we forget Prof. Sam Bergman. Twenty years ago, Sam returned to teaching at George Washington University in the United States and has been living there ever since. At the beginning of 2017, I wanted to renew contact with him in order to let him know about the implications of his act of Tikkun Olam and about the writing of this book. With great excitement, I composed this e-mail:

Dear Sam,

I hope this message finds you and your family in good health and spirits.

It has been long since we have talked or met. I would be very happy to meet with you soon. As you know, I have been active in Philanthropy in Israel for many years. In 2004 along with my friends, I established a non-profit organization called "Ofanim" which provides children and youth extracurricular classes in Science Technology and Math. "Ofanim" operates in small and remote communities in the north and south of the country. "Ofanim" was established to a large extent thanks to you - following the positive experience I had with you during my childhood. You may not know it, but you became a very essential and significant figure in my life. Our first meeting at lunch at my late parents' house greatly influenced me and greatly shaped my future. The experiences we try to create for the children in "Ofanim" are based on the empowering experience I had with you. The idea is to strengthen the children's confidence, sense of self-efficacy and to break the artificial obstacles that have been imposed on them, thereby making academic studies achievable and accessible to them. You have good reason to be proud of the results of your actions.

Over the last few years, I have talked a lot about the experience that led me to social involvement and the establishment of the non-profit organization "Ofanim". I spoke a great deal about you and the central role you played in my life. About three years ago, I decided to write a book about social action, involvement and giving in Israel. I just recently finished writing it. I am currently working on editing the book and hope it will be published within a few months. The first chapter of the book opens with the description of our first encounter at my parents' home when you came for lunch, the first six private lessons you gave me at the university when I was 14, and especially the tremendous impact of these meetings on my life.

To close a circle for me and for the readers of the book, I thought I would be honored if I could incorporate your point of view of these meetings into the book. In any case, it would be a great pleasure for me to personally present you with a copy of the book once it is published.

With much appreciation,
Haim

He replied soon after:

Dear Haim,

I was very happy to have received your message. Regarding your book, I'm very flattered that I rate so highly in your life assessment. My point of view differs somewhat... while your success is in part due to mentoring and opportunity that is not available to many kids in far-flung regions in the world in general and in the south of Israel in particular, you must realize that success has many components. I found you, the fourteen-year-old, a kid with amazing motivation, desire to learn, perseverance and the ability to work hard – an unbeatable combination. Nonetheless, the organization you founded (Ofanim) is a remarkable payback and a great boon to Israeli society, one you can be very proud of, as am I!

Incidentally, yesterday I celebrated my 80th birthday and had a long Skype conversation with my children and grandchildren from India, Los

Angeles, Israel and England. Isn't technology great sometimes?

Yours,
Sam

Immediately after receiving his reply, we spoke on the telephone and arranged to meet a few weeks later in the United States. I felt like there was no better, more meaningful and worthy gift that I could present to this humble and beloved man than the fruits of his Tikkun Olam act for his 80th birthday.

# EPILOGUE

As one who has experienced the implications of Tikkun Olam on both sides, as the recipient and the giver, I believe with all my heart that through our actions — even the smallest ones — we have the power to repair our world and the world of the weak and needy among us: the world of a child, of a youth, of an elderly person, of a Holocaust survivor, of a disabled person and more. By joining the circle of social involvement, action and giving — in the individual acts of Tikkun Olam of each one of us — we can serve as a light that illuminates the darkness of the world of others. A light that has the power to do wonders. "The miracle of the light," wrote Emmanuel Levinas, "is that it is richer than the energies feeding it... It is the daily marvel of the spirit... It is a flame that burns with its own fervor... the will that undertakes to do something despite the paralyzing obstacles in its way; the hope that lights up a life... It concerns the infinite resources of the spirit that, as a creator, surpasses the prudence of techniques; without calculation, without past, it joyfully pours forth its feelings in space, freely and prodigiously entering into the cause of the Other."[3]

As we have joined our small light of action into the torch

of social action in Israel, with our joint power we are able to illuminate society as a whole and bring about fundamental and significant social changes, which today might seem to us to be but a distant dream. This belief doesn't stem from naivety — although naivety is sometimes necessary in order to dream big — but from the recognition of the tremendous rewards that one little touch of grace can bring about.

# ACKNOWLEDGEMENTS

This book is another small link in the chain of the amazing social action that is being done in Israel. It's the work of wonderful people and well-meaning organizations who work day and night for the advancement of society in Israel. In writing this book I have been helped by many of these wonderful people, for whom social involvement and social action are a way of life. These amazing people are inspirational and set an example of social commitment and taking action for the sake of others.

First of all, I would like to thank from the bottom of my heart my partners in the social journey and in the "pure space" — members of the past and present board of directors of Ofanim: Adv. Yoni Abadi, Ronen Barel, Dr. Yigal Ben Shalom, Rimon Ben Shaul, Yoel Caraso, Dr. Gadi Cwengel, Roni Freidman, Yaacov Goldman, Oded Hadomi, Avi Harrari, Giddy Hollander, Mario Meschiany, Poly Meschiany, Aviya Oleiski, Alon Piltz, Jimmy Pinto, Dr. Michael Reiner, Dr. Adam Reuter, Dr. Tamar Shifter, Dr. Shiran Sivanei, Prof. Gad Yair, Major General (reserve duty) Yoram Yair (Ya Ya) , Rafi Zarfati; to Yoram Gonen — my friend and partner on the way to founding Ofanim — for the consistency, the support, the loyalty and the strong friendship; to my dear friend, Yaakov Iluz, for the wise counsel, the precise and professional reading of the text, and the important notes and highlights. This book contains insights on giving and a deep personal commitment and devotion to others that I have learned from each and every one of you.

Special thanks to the real Ofans (angels), each and every member of the board of directors of Friends of Ofanim in the United States: Ed Baumstein, Angelica Berrie, Arie Cohen, Jacob Engel, Mark Fishman, Ken Goldblatt, Charles Gwirtsman, Faye Kimerling, Ben Kirschner, Ari Kushner, Toren Kutnick, Henry Levi z"l, Amy Lipton z"l, Ruth Newman, Tamar Oded, David Rich, Yoav Shiffman, Paul Silberberg, Bob Wiener, Peter Wright and all of the amazingly generous supporters of Ofanim. With your generosity and your tremendous commitment to the children of Israel, you symbolize the true essence of mutual responsibility that is embodied in our tradition of "Kol Israel Arevim Ze-La Ze."

To Eli Dror, Yasmin Zarchin-Elad, Adir Khan, Mor Limonad, the instructors, drivers, managers and professional staff of the Ofanim family in the past and present: your true and sincere concern for the children of Israel is Zionism at its best. As we say, "Blessed is the nation that these are its sons."

To Shirley, my beloved wife, partner and best friend: with great patience, you have given attention to every sentence and every passage of this book countless times. In your wisdom you have advised, commented and enlightened me on the way to the successful conclusion of this writing project. This book would not have been published without your substantial contribution.

To my beloved children: Amit, Shani, Hanoi, Yaniv and Elia. I love, cherish and appreciate each and every one of you. It is important that you know that this book is truly for you. I am sure you will be able to find your unique path of social action, involvement and giving.

To Dov Eichenwald and Yediot Books Publications; to Benny Carmi and eBookPro, thank you for your assistance in making this publication possible. To Dina Saadon — I could not have asked for a more professional, talented and patient translator than you. Thank you very much.

# NOTES

## Chapter One

1. Gad Yair: "From Key Experiences to Turning Points: A Study of Educational Impact" [Hebrew], Sifriat Poalim Publishing group - Hakibbutz Hameuchad -, 2006
2. Pirkei Avot 3:15
3. Max Born "Man and the Atom," Bulletin Of The Atomic Scientists Vol. 13, Iss. 6,1957.
4. Eyal Bar-Haim, Carmel Blank, Yossi Shavit: "Educational Opportunity, Employment, and Income: 1995-2008", Taub Center for Social Policy Studies in Israel, 2013.
5. See note number 4.

## Chapter Two

1. Central Bureau of Statistics: "Gross Domestic Product and Uses of Resources in 1995-2015" [Hebrew], 2016.
2. Central Bureau of Statistics: "Education at a Glance 2013: OECD Indicators", 2013.
3. Central Bureau of Statistics: "Society in Israel Report -Number

5, Chapter 1: Welfare of the population, employment and living conditions" [Hebrew], 2012.

4. Chana Bar-Ishai and Peer-Li Fior: "The education system in Israel in comparison to countries of the world" [Hebrew], 2009.

5. Central Bureau of Statistics: "National Expenditure on Education in 2009-2012" [Hebrew], 2013.

6. Dan Ben David, "The State of Israel's Education and Its Implications," Taub Center for Social Policy Studies in Israel, 2011.

7. PISA Results: "Chapter 7, Achieving Problem Solving Skills in PISA study 2015" [Hebrew], 2015.

8. TIMSS Study, 2015.

9. Central Bureau of Statistics: "Meitzav exam results according to socio-economic strata" [Hebrew], 2003.

10. www.eduaction.co.li: "Five Unit Mathematics: A strategy that created a strategic threat" [Hebrew], August 2015.

11. Walla website: "A 27 percent rise in Five Unit Mathematics matriculation exams in 2016" [Hebrew], June 7, 2016, http://news.walla.co.il/ item/2968209

12. Haaretz website: "Meitzav data 5776: For the first time ever, there's a narrowing of the gaps between population strata in some of the subjects" [Hebrew], November 15, 2016. http://www.haaretz.co.il/news/education/1.3122948

13. Idit Mani-Ikan et al.: "Teaching Five Study Unit Mathematics in Arab Society" [Hebrew], Henrietta Szold Institute, September 2016.

14. McKinsey et al.: "How the world's best performing schools come out on top," 2007.

15. Paul Anthony Samuelson: "Foundations of Economic Analysis," 1946 (1973).

16. The Knesset: A description and analysis of the poverty and inequality indexes in Israel and the developed countries" [Hebrew], Research and Information Center, Budgetary Control Department, 2012.

17. Adi Schwartz, "Third-world? Us?" [Hebrew], the Haaretz website, April 20, 2007.

18. Bank of Israel Report: "Chapter 8 - Issues in Welfare Policy" [Hebrew], 2013.

19. The Knesset: "A description and analysis of the poverty and inequality indices in Israel and the developed countries" [Hebrew], Research and Information Center, Budgetary Control Department, 2012.

20. National Insurance Institute of Israel: "Poverty Indices and the Social Gaps, Annual Report 2014," Director General of Research and Planning, December 2015.

21. Central Bureau of Statistics: "Society in Israel Report -Number 5. Chapter 2: Poverty and social exclusion in comparison to other EU countries" [Hebrew], 2012.

22. UNICEF Report 2015.

23. Momi Dahan, "Third generation poverty" [Hebrew], The Israel Democracy Institute website, 2009.

24. John Gal and Shavit Madhala-Brik: "Public Spending on Social Welfare," The Taub Center for Social Policy Studies in Israel, 2016.

25. The Knesset: "A description and analysis of the poverty and inequality indexes in Israel and the developed countries" [Hebrew], Research and Information Center, Budgetary Control Department, 2012.

26. Guy Rolnik: "Stuck in the status- If your grandfather was poor, also you, your children and your grandchildren won't finish the

month" [Hebrew], The Marker, February 15, 2014.

27. Credit Suisse: "Global Wealth Report," 2015.

28. Jacob Hacker and Paul Pierson: "Winner-Take-All Politics," 2010.

29. Galit Ben Naim and Alexey Belinsky: "Israel's Wage Divergence: An Analysis of Wage Mobility in the Last Decade" [Hebrew], 2010.'

30. Moshe Halbertal: "Shabbat Supplement" Yediot Ahronot, Interview with Nahum Barnea [Hebrew], August 26, 2016.

31. Momi Dahan: "How successful was the melting pot in the economic field?", Israel Democracy. Institute, 2013.

32. State of Human Rights Report: "The right to health: Plans to narrow gaps between the center and the periphery", Situation Report, 2012.

33. State Comptroller's Report: "Annual Report (63c) for 2012" [Hebrew], 2013.

34. Tali Marom and Zvi Eckstein: "Position Paper: Poverty in Israel, Reasons and Policies in the Labor Market" [Hebrew], 2016.

35. National Insurance Institute of Israel: "Poverty Indexes and the Social Gaps, Annual Report 2014," Director General of Research and Planning, December 2015.

36. Sheleg Bambi, "Liba V'Liboey" [Hebrew], Yedioth Aharonot, July 2016.

37. Yoaz Hendel: "Yofi Hablorit Ve-hatoar HaRishon" [Hebrew], Yedioth Aharonot, August 2916.

38. Rami Sulimani: "The importance of social resilience for the national security of the State of Israel [Hebrew]", In the framework of Israel's National Security Seminar - Challenge and Response, 2014.

39. See note number 38.

40. Stephen Hawking: "This is the most dangerous time for our planet", The Guardian, December 1st, 2016, https://www.theguardian.com/commentisfree/2016/dec/01/stephen-hawking-dangerous-time-planet-inequality?CMP=share_btn_link

41. Robert I. Fitzhenry: "The Harper Book of Quotations," p. 356, 1993.

42. Maimonides: "The Guide for the Perplexed," Part A, Chapter 31.

43. S.Y. Agnon: "Shira," 1971.

44. Rabbi Abraham Joshua Heschel: "God Believes in Man," 2011.

45. Benjamin Kidron, Hagai Katz and Mihal Bar: "The Third Sector in Israel: Between Welfare State and Civilian Society" [Hebrew], Hakibbutz Hameuchad Publishing, 2003.

46. Yaakov Rotblit and HaHazer HaAchorit: "Song of the Poor" [Hebrew], 2013.

47. See note number 44.

48. The Dalai Lama: "The Compassionate Life"

49. Dr. Dana Freibach-Heifetz: "Secular Grace" [Hebrew], 2009.

50. Richard Dawkins "The Selfish Gene," 1991.

51. Rabbi Abraham Joshua Heschel: "The Plight of Russian Jews," United Synagogue Review, 1964.

52. See note number 44.

53. Rabbi Yuval Cherlow: "Avar Liva LeIsha Meleva" [Hebrew], "Amit Orot HaTorah" homepage, February 4, 2016.

54. Rabbi Shlomo Ishon: "A free economy that educates to give" [Hebrew], from the Komemiut movement's weekly newsletter, the 28th of Iyar, 5769, 2009.

55. Maimonides: "Mishne Torah - The Laws of the Gifts to be Given to the Poor," Chapter 10, Halacha 14 and onward.

56. Shimon Peres: A speech to the participants of the JNF

Conference in Tel Aviv, 2012. https://www.youtube.com/watch?v=YNxN8rD5T_E&feature=youtu.be

57. Maimonides: "Mishne Torah - The Book of Knowledge" Hilchot Teshuvah, Chapter 3, Halacha 5.

58. Albert Einstein: "Religion and Science," New York Times, 1930.

59. Jennifer Aaker, et al.: "Getting the Most out of Giving: Concretely Framing a Prosocial Goal Maximizes Happiness", 2013.

60. Central Bureau of Statistics: "Selected Data from the Social Survey 2013 Volunteering in Israel on the occasion of International Volunteer Day," 2013.

61. "Plato's Writings," Libs translation, Shoken Publishing, Volume I — Epilogue, pg. 223.

62. Joel Hansel: Introduction to "Totality and Infinity," 2010.

63. Emmanuel Levinas: "Totality and Infinity," 2010.

64. Haim Shapira: "Nocturnal Musings: Kierkegaard, Schopenhauer, Nietzsche", 2011.

## CHAPTER THREE

1. Albert Einstein: "Religion and Science," New York Times, 1930.

2. Yoram Yuval: "*Heshbon Nefesh*" [Hebrew], an article on Ynet, August 19, 2016.

3. Hillel Schmid: "Characteristics of the Israeli Philanthropy in the 21st Century," June 2011.

4. Marcel Mauss: "The Gift: The form and reason for exchange in archaic societies," Introduction by I. Silber: "On Marcel Mauss and the Gift's Charms and Paradoxes," pg. 7-30, 2005.

5. Aristotle: "Nicomachean Ethics", Book II

6. Central Bureau of Statistics: "Road Accidents" {[Hebrew], Statistical Abstract of Israel, 2017.

7. *Perkei Avot*, Chapter 2, *Mishneh* 4.

8. See source number 3.

9. Jeffry A. Krames: "Lead with Humility," American Management Association, 2012.

10. Ministry of Justice: "Registered Non-profit Organizations Database" [Hebrew], Non-profit Organizations Registrar website, 2015.

11. GuideStar – NPTech: "Non-profit organizations in Israel abstract" [Hebrew], August 2014.

12. Ministry of Justice: "Summary of data from the GuideStar Conference" [Hebrew], Registrar of Nonprofit Organizations website, http://index.justice.gov.il/Pubilcations/.26.6.12 Articles/Pages/KeneshMigzarSlisi.aspx

13. Central Bureau of Statistics: "Israeli Philanthropy Survey 2009 — 2011", March 2014.

14. Haim Nachman Bialik: "*HaShirim,*" Dvir Publishing Ltd., 2004.

15. Ministry of Interior: "Publication of local authorities in Israel 2012: The local authorities in Israel in cooperation with Central Bureau of Statistics" [Hebrew], 2012.

16. Central Bureau of Statistics: "Socio-economic ranking relative to population size" [Hebrew], 2002.

17. Yaron Drokman and Avital Lahav: "The socio-economic ranking: Savion in first place" [Hebrew], ynet, April 3, 2013.

18. Central Bureau of Statistics: "Characterization and Classification of Local Authorities by the Socio-Economic Level of the Population" [Hebrew], 1999.

19. See note number 18.

20. Yehonatan Almog: "Narrowing the digital divide — the use of computers in the education system in Israel" [Hebrew], The Hebrew University - The Federmann School of Public Policy and Government, 2008.

21. Roey Goldschmidt: Narrowing the Digital Gap" [Hebrew], The Knesset — Research and Development Center, 2007.

22. Tractate Sanhedrin, Chapter 4, Mishneh 5

23. Netanel Katz: "Defining a vision and its foundation: a cornerstone for quality leadership" [Hebrew], 2000.

## Chapter Four

1. William G. Domhoff: "The Power Elite and Their Challengers: The Role of American Behavior Scientist", Nonprofits in American Social Conflict, 2009.

2. F. Ostrower: "Why the wealthy give: The culture of elite philanthropy", Princeton N.J., Princeton University Press. Introduction, pp. 3-27. 1995.

3. Ministry of Justice: "Proper management of non-profit organizations" [Hebrew], Third Edition 2013.

4. Eliyah Tannenbaum: "Building ability — the next stage: A director's course for members of the board of directors" [Hebrew], http://marompb.com/articles, September 2016.

5. Daniel Milo: "Member of the public administration, ethics and practice" [Hebrew], The Jerusalem Center for Ethics, 2015.

6. See note number 3.

7. Jeffrey A. Sonnenfeld: "What Makes Great Boards Great," Harvard Business Review, September 2002.

8. Ministry of Justice: "Guidelines for Managing Non-profit Organizations" [Hebrew], Non-profit Organizations Registrar, December 2015.

9. Richard P. Chait, et al.: "Governance as Leadership: Reframing the Work of Nonprofit Boards", 2005.

10. See note number 8.

11. BDO Ziv Haft: "The NGO and Social Business sector," The shortened guide for NGO 4, updated version, 2016.

12. See note number 7.

13. See note number 9.

14. See note number 7.

15. Ezekiel 1:21.

## Chapter Five

1. Hillel Schmid, Avishag Rudich: "Elite Philanthropy in Israel: Characteristics, Motives and Patterns of Contribution" [Hebrew], Social Security, 2009.

2. See note number 1.

3. Ministry of Justice: "Summary of data from the GuideStar Conference" [Hebrew], Registrar of Nonprofit Organizations website, June 26, 2012.

4. Ministry of Justice: "Registered Non-profit Organizations Database" [Hebrew], Non-profit Organizations Registrar website, 2015.

5. NPTech: "Non-profit organizations in Israel abstract" [Hebrew], 2014.

6. Committed to Give and Central Bureau of Statistics survey: "Philanthropy of Israelis, 2009-2011," 2014.

7. Charities Aid Foundation: "World Giving Index," www. cafonline. org, 2014 and 2015.

8. MATAN survey: "They value the non-profit organizations but don't donate to them" [Hebrew], Calcalist supplement, June 22, 2016.

9. TPI: "Promoting Philanthropy in Israel," 2008.

10. Ilana Friedrich Silber et al.: "Civil Society and Third Sector in Israel," 2008.

11. Daniel Milo: "Member of Public Administration, the ethics and the practice" [Hebrew], The Jerusalem Ethics Center, 2015.

12. Ministry of Justice: "Proper management of non-profit organizations" [Hebrew], Third Edition 2013.

13. Hillel Schmid: "Characteristics of the Israeli Philanthropy in the 21st Century," June 2011.

14. Giving USA: "The Annual Report on Philanthropy for the Year 2015" Chicago: Giving USA Foundation™, 2016.

15. Central Bureau of Statistics: "Expenditures and Income of Non-Profit Institutions 2012-2014" [Hebrew], 2015.

16. See note number 5

17. Central Bureau of Statistics: "Israeli Philanthropy Survey 2009 — 2011" [Hebrew], March 2014.

18. Ministry of Justice website: "Summary of data from the GuideStar Conference" [Hebrew], Registrar of Nonprofit Organizations, June 26, 2012.

19. Knesset Information and Research Center: "Government support in public institutions," 2010.

20. Attorney General's guidelines for the government, guideline no. 1.2005: "State support for public institutions under Section 3A of the Israeli Foundations of the Budget Law" [Hebrew], 2005.

21. See note number 17.

22. See note number 6.

23. The Institute for Law and Philanthropy, The Buchmann Faculty of Law, Tel Aviv University: "Household Giving Patterns in Israel, 2016," March 2017.

24. See note number 6.

25. Credit Suisse: "The Credit Suisse Research Institute's Global Wealth Report" [Hebrew], 2015. http://www.themarker.com/wallstreet/1.2750668

26. See note number 23.

27. See note number 14.

28. See note number 14.

29. AFP - Association for Fundraising Professionals: "2016 Fundraising Effectiveness Survey Report," 2016.

30. Bloomberg: "A Guide to Donor Retention" https://bloomerang.co/retention8, 2016.

## Chapter Six

1. Friedman Milton: "The social responsibility of business is to increase its profits," New York Times, September 1970.

2. Liad Arthur: "Requiring companies to report on social and environmental issues" [Hebrew], The Marker, June 18, 2013.

3. Moran Harari et al.: "The Missing Billions: Aggressive Tax Planning and Corporate Social Responsibility in Israel", The College of Law and Business — The Corporate Social Responsibility Clinic, 2011.

4. Inbal Abu: "Social Responsibility of Social Organizations" [Hebrew], Ben Gurion University, April 2013.

5. See note number 3.

6. See note number 4.

7. Infospot website: "New legislation requires publication of a corporate responsibility report in Europe. What's in Israel?" [Hebrew], March 13, 2016.

8. Infospot website: "2015 Annual summary of corporate responsibility reports" [Hebrew], February 25, 2016.

9. See note number 4.

10. Maala website: http://www.maala.org.il, September 2016.

11. Committed to Give and Central Bureau of Statistics survey: "Israeli Philanthropy Survey 2009 — 2011", March 2014.

12. William Foster et al.: "Making Big Bets for Social Change," Stanford Social Innovation Review, Winter 2016.

13. Silberberg Paul: "The Ethical Entrepreneur: Succeeding in business without Selling your Soul", 2017.

14. Hillel Schmid: "Characteristics of the Israeli Philanthropy in the 21st Century," June 2011.

15. N. Brennar et al.: "Survey of Philanthropic Foundations and Funding Institutions in Israel" [Hebrew], The Center for the Study of Philanthropy in Israel — The Hebrew University in Jerusalem, 2010.

16. See note number 11.

17. See note number 14.

18. Hillel Schmid et al.: ""The Globalization of Philanthropy: Means, Channels and Giving of the Diaspora", The Center for the Study of Philanthropy in Israel — The Hebrew University in Jerusalem, 2013.

19. A Non-profit Organization Registrar booklet on the matter

"Proper Management of Non-profit Organizations" [Hebrew], December 2015.

20. See note number 19.

21. Ministry of Justice: "The third addition to the Companies Law - Ways of Investing a Public Benefit Fund" [Hebrew], 2014.

## Chapter Seven

1. Anita M. Baker: "Participatory Evaluation Essentials An Updated Guide for Nonprofit Organizations and Their Evaluation Partners," The Bruner Foundation, 2010.

2. See note 1.

3. Fay Twersky et al.: "Measurement and Evaluation in the Israeli Non-Profit Sector," International Advisory Committee, Yad Hanadiv, October 2010.

4. Midot website: www.midot.org.il, 2016.

5. See note number 3.

6. See note number 3.

7. See note number 1.

8. See note number 3.

9. See note number 1.

10. Janice M. Morse et al.: "Criteria for Concept Evaluation," Journal of Advance Nursing, 1996.

11. Stefano Campostrini: "Measurement and Effectiveness: Methodologies Considerations, Issues and Possible Solutions", Chapter 18, 2005.

## Conclusion

1. Albert Einstein: "The World As I See It" [Hebrew], A. Y. Stybel Publishing, 5695.
2. Rabbi Yosef Dov HaLevi Soloveitchik: "The Community" from Devrei Hagut v'Haracha, Jerusalem, 1982.
3. Emmanuel Levinas, "Difficult Freedom," 1967.

# LIST OF RIGHTS OWNERS

# ABOUT THE AUTHOR

Haim Dahan is a high-tech entrepreneur who founded and served as chairman and CEO of several technology companies including A.S.Y.D. Investments Ltd. and Kaizen Bio-Tech (2011) Ltd. Haim is also the founder and president of "Ofanim - For the Advancement of Children and Youth in Israel" and a member of the "Friends of Ofanim" organization in the United States. In addition to his philanthropic involvement in Ofanim, he serves on the board of directors of several technology companies and of various organizations including "Committed to Give", the Jewish Funders Network in Israel, and the global Jewish Funders Network (JFN). He was awarded "Most Effective Private Social Investor" for 2013 by the public awards granting committee of Midot, an organization headed by president emeritus of the Israeli Supreme Court, Meir Shamgar. Haim is co-author of *Proactive Data Mining with Decision Trees*, a book on proactive data mining methods.

Haim is married to Shirley and the father of Amit, Shani, Hanoy, Yaniv, and Eliya. He holds bachelor's and master's degrees from the Department of Computer Science and Mathematics at Ben-Gurion University and a Ph.D. in engineering from Tel Aviv University.